D1170587

SIX

WALKS

IN THE

FICTIONAL

WOODS

UMBERTO ECO

SIX
WALKS
IN THE
FICTIONAL
WOODS

HARVARD
UNIVERSITY
PRESS
Cambridge
Massachusetts
and London
England

Copyright © 1994 by the President and
Fellows of Harvard College
All rights reserved
Printed in the United States of America

FOURTH PRINTING, 1995

First Harvard University Press paperback
edition, 1995

"Scenes We'd Like to See: The Musketeer
Who Failed to Get the Girl," by Phil
Interlandi, is from *Mad* magazine no. 27,
© 1955 by E. C. Publications, Inc., and is
used with permission.

*Library of Congress Cataloging-in-
Publication Data*
Eco, Umberto.
Six walks in the fictional woods /
Umberto Eco.
p. cm.—(The Charles Eliot Norton
lectures; 1993)
Includes index.
ISBN 0-674-81050-3 (cloth)
ISBN 0-674-81051-1 (pbk.)
1. Fiction—Technique. 2. Narration
(Rhetoric) 3. Nerval, Gérard de, 1808-1855.
Sylvie. I. Title. II. Series.
PN3355.E28   1994
808.3—dc20

93-33605
CIP

CONTENTS

1 ENTERING THE WOODS   1

2 THE WOODS OF LOISY   27

3 LINGERING IN THE WOODS   49

4 POSSIBLE WOODS   75

5 THE STRANGE CASE
OF THE RUE SERVANDONI   97

6 FICTIONAL PROTOCOLS   117

NOTES   143

INDEX   149

ONE

ENTERING THE WOODS

I would like to begin by evoking the memory of Italo Calvino, who eight years ago was invited to give his six Norton lectures but who had time to write only five of them before leaving us. I evoke him not merely as my friend but also as the author of *If on a Winter's Night a Traveler,* because his novel is concerned with the presence of the reader in the story and my lectures will to a great extent be devoted to the same subject.

In the same year that Calvino's book came out in Italy, one of my own books was published—namely, *Lector in fabula,* which corresponds only in part to the English version, *The Role of the Reader.* The English and Italian titles of this work are different because, if the Italian (or Latin) title were translated literally into English, it would be "The Reader in the Fairy Tale," which means nothing. In Italy the expression "Lupus in fabula" is the equivalent of "Speak of the devil," and is used when an individual whom people have just been talking about suddenly turns up. But whereas the Italian expression summons the wolf, which appears in all folktales, I refer instead to the reader. Indeed, the wolf may not even figure in many situations, and we shall soon see that in its place there could be an ogre. But in a story there is always a reader, and this reader is a fundamental ingredient not only of the process of storytelling but also of the tale itself.

Today, anyone who compared my *Lector in fabula* with *If on a Winter's Night a Traveler* might think that my book was a response to Calvino's novel. But the two works came out at about the same time and neither of us knew what the other was doing, even though for a long time we had both been deeply preoccupied with the same problems. When Calvino sent me his book, he had certainly already received mine, since his dedication reads, "A Umberto: superior stabat lector, longeque inferior Italo Calvino." The quotation is obviously adapted from Phaedrus' fable about the wolf and the lamb ("Superior stabat lupus, longeque inferior agnus," or "The wolf was upstream and the lamb downstream"), and Calvino was alluding to my *Lector in fabula*. But the phrase "longeque inferior," which means both "downstream" and "inferior" or "less important," is still referentially ambiguous. If the word "lector" is to be taken *de dicto* as designating my book, Calvino was either choosing an ironically humble role or proudly taking on the positive one of the lamb, leaving the theorist with that of the Big Bad Wolf. If, on the contrary, the word "lector" is to be taken *de re* and meant the Reader, Calvino was making a major statement and was paying homage to the role of the reader.

To pay homage to Calvino, I shall take as my starting point the second of Calvino's *Six Memos for the Next Millennium*[1] (his Norton lectures), the "memo" dedicated to quickness, in which he refers to the fifty-seventh tale in his anthology *Italian Folktales*:

> A king fell ill and was told by his doctors, "Majesty, if you want to get well, you'll have to obtain one of the ogre's feathers. That will not be easy, since the ogre eats every human he sees."
>
> The king passed the word on to everybody, but no one was willing to go to the ogre. Then he asked one of his most loyal and courageous attendants, who said, "I will go."
>
> The man was shown the road and told, "On a mountaintop are seven caves, in one of which lives the ogre."[2]

Calvino remarks that "not a word is said about what illness the king was suffering from, or why on earth an ogre should have feathers, or what those caves were like," and he praises the quality of swiftness in a narrative, although he asserts that "this apologia for quickness does not presume to deny the pleasures of lingering."[3] I shall devote my third lecture to lingering. For the moment, let us note that any narrative fiction is necessarily and fatally swift because, in building a world that comprises myriad events and characters, it cannot say everything about this world. It hints at it and then asks the reader to fill in a whole series of gaps. Every text, after all (as I have already written), is a lazy machine asking the reader to do some of its work. What a problem it would be if a text were to say everything the receiver is to understand—it would never end. If I were to phone you and say, "I'll take the highway and be with you in an hour," you would not expect me to add that I shall use my car along with the highway.

In *Agosto, moglie mia non ti conosco,* the great comic writer Achille Campanile wrote the following dialogue:

Gedeone gestured wildly to a carriage standing at the end of the street. The elderly coachman climbed down from the driver's seat with difficulty and walked as quickly as he could toward our friends, saying, "How can I help you?"

"No!" cried Gedeone irritably, "I want the carriage!"

"Oh!" replied the coachman with disappointment, "I thought you wanted me."

He returned to the carriage, climbed into the driver's box, and asked Gedeone, who had taken his seat in the vehicle along with Andrea: "Where to?"

"I can't tell you," said Gedeone, who wanted to keep his expedition a secret. The coachman, who was not very inquisitive, did not persist. They all sat motionless for a few minutes, looking at the view. In the end, Gedeone, unable to control himself any longer, exclaimed, "To Fiorenzina castle!"—which made the horse start and led the coachman to protest, "At this time of day? We'll get there after nightfall."

"That's true," muttered Gedeone. "We'll go tomorrow morning. Come and collect us at seven o'clock sharp."

"In the carriage?" inquired the coachman. Gedeone reflected for a few minutes. Finally he said, "Yes, that would be better."

As he was heading back to the inn he turned and shouted to the coachman, "Hey! Don't forget the horse!"

"Are you serious?" said the other man in surprise. "Well, as you wish."[4]

The passage is absurd because the protagonists at first say less than they should and in the end feel the urge to say (and hear) what it is not necessary to say.

At times, in wanting to say too much, an author may become more comic than his or her characters. A very popular writer in nineteenth-century Italy was Carolina Invernizio, who nourished the dreams of whole generations of proletarians with stories such as *A Dead Woman's Kiss, A Madwoman's Revenge,* and *The Accusing Corpse.* Carolina Invernizio wrote quite badly, and my translation will be rather faithful. It has been remarked that she had the courage, or the weakness, to introduce into literature the language of the petty bureaucracy of the newly formed Italian state (a bureaucracy to which her husband, manager of a military bakery, belonged). This is how Carolina begins her novel *The Murderous Inn:*

> It was a beautiful evening, even if it was very cold. The streets of Turin were illuminated as if by daylight by the moon high in the sky. The station clock showed seven o'clock. Under the large porch a deafening noise could be heard because two nonstop trains were meeting. One about to leave, the other about to arrive.[5]

We should not be too hard on Mrs. Invernizio. She somehow felt that speed is a great narrative virtue, but she could never have begun, as Kafka did (in his "Metamorphosis"), with the sentence: "As Gregor Samsa awoke one morning from uneasy dreams he found himself transformed in his bed into a gigantic insect."[6] Her readers would have immediately asked her how and why Gregor Samsa had become an insect and what he had eaten the day before. Incidentally, Alfred Kazin relates that Thomas Mann lent one of Kafka's novels to Einstein, who gave it back to him saying: "I couldn't read it; the human mind isn't that complex."[7]

Einstein was perhaps complaining that the story was rather slow (but I shall later praise the art of slowing down). Indeed, the reader does not always know how to collaborate with the speed of the text. In *Reading and Understanding,* Roger Schank tells us another story:

> John loved Mary but she didn't want to marry him. One day, a dragon stole Mary from the castle. John got on top of his horse and killed the dragon. Mary agreed to marry him. They lived happily ever after.[8]

In this book Schank is concerned with what children understand when they read, and he asked a three-year-old girl about the story.

P: Why did John kill the dragon?

C: 'Cause it was mean.

P: What was mean about it?

C: It was hurting him.

P: How did it hurt him?

C: It was probably throwing fire at him.

P: Why did Mary agree to marry John?

C: 'Cause she loved him very much and he wanted very much to marry her . . .

P: How come Mary decided to marry John when she wouldn't in the beginning?

C: That's a hard question.

P: Well, what do you think the answer is?

C: Because then she just didn't want him and then he argued very much and talked to her a lot about marrying her and then she got interested in marrying her, I mean him.

Evidently, the girl's knowledge of the world included the fact that dragons breathe flames from their nostrils but not that you can yield, out of gratitude or admiration, to a love you do not reciprocate. A story may be more or less quick—that is to say, more or less elliptic—but how elliptic it may be is determined by the sort of reader it is addressed to.

Since I try to justify all the titles I have been foolish enough to choose for my works, let me also justify the title of my Norton lectures. Woods are a metaphor for the narrative text, not only for the text of fairy tales but for any narrative text. There are woods like Dublin, where instead of Little Red Riding Hood one can meet Molly Bloom, and woods like Casablanca, in which one can meet Ilsa Lund or Rick Blaine.

To use a metaphor devised by Jorge Luis Borges (another spirit who is very much present in these talks and who gave his own Norton lectures twenty-five years ago), a wood is a garden of forking paths. Even when there are no well-trodden paths in a wood, everyone can trace his or her own path, deciding to go to the left or to the right of a certain tree and making a choice at every tree encountered.

In a narrative text, the reader is forced to make choices all the time. Indeed, this obligation to choose is found even at the level of the individual sentence—at least, every time a transitive verb occurs. Whenever the speaker is about to end a sentence, we as readers or listeners make a bet (albeit unconsciously): we predict his or her choice, or anxiously wonder what choice will be made (at least in the case of dramatic sentences such as "Last night in the graveyard of the vicarage I saw . . .").

Sometimes the narrator wants to leave us free to imagine how the story will continue. Let's look, for example, at the end of Poe's *Narrative of Arthur Gordon Pym*:

And now we rushed into the embraces of the cataract, where a chasm threw itself open to receive us. But there arose in our pathway a shrouded human figure, very far larger in its proportions than any dweller among men. And the hue of the skin of the figure was of the perfect whiteness of the snow.

Here, where the voice of the narrator ceases, the author wants us to spend the rest of our lives wondering what happened; and fearing that we are not yet consumed by the desire to know what will never be revealed to us, the author, not the voice of the narrator, adds a note at the end telling us that, after the disappearance of Mr. Pym, "the few remaining chapters which were to complete his narration . . . have been irrecoverably lost." We shall never escape from that wood—as happened, for instance, to Jules Verne, Charles Romyn Dake, and H. P. Lovecraft, who decided to stay in there by trying to continue Pym's story.

But there are cases in which the author wants sadistically to show us that we are not Stanley but Livingstone, and that we are doomed to get lost in the woods by continuing to make the wrong choices. Take Laurence Sterne, right at the beginning of *Tristram Shandy*:

> I wish either my father or my mother, or indeed both of them, as they were in duty both equally bound to it, had minded what they were about when they begot me; had they duly consider'd how much depended upon what they were then doing . . .

What can the Shandy couple have been doing at that delicate moment? In order to leave the reader time to think out some reasonable predictions (even the most embarrassing ones), Sterne digresses for a whole paragraph (which shows that Calvino was right not to disdain the art of lingering), after which he reveals the mistake that was made in the primal scene:

> *Pray, my dear*, quoth my mother, *have you not forgot to wind up the clock?*——*Good G—!* cried my father, making an exclamation, but taking care to moderate his voice at the same time,——*Did ever woman, since the creation of the world, interrupt a man with such a silly question?*

As you can see, the father thinks of the mother exactly what the reader thinks of Sterne. Was there ever an author, however evil minded, who so frustrated his readers?

Certainly, after Sterne, avant-garde narrative has often tried not only to upset our expectations as readers but even to create readers who expect complete freedom of choice from the book they are reading. Yet this freedom can be enjoyed precisely because—on the strength of a tradition thousands of years old, comprising narratives ranging from primitive myths to the modern detective novel—readers are generally willing to make their own choices in the narrative wood on the assumption that some will be more reasonable than others.

I say "reasonable" as if these were choices based on common sense. But it would be wrong to assume that a book of fiction is read according to common sense. It is certainly not what is asked of us by Sterne or Poe or even by the author (if there originally was one) of "Little Red Riding Hood." In fact, common sense would make us reject the idea that the wood contains a wolf that talks. So what do I mean when I say that in the narrative wood the reader must make reasonable choices?

At this point I must refer to two concepts that I have already discussed elsewhere—namely, those of the Model Reader and the Model Author.[9]

The model reader of a story is not the empirical reader. The empirical reader is you, me, anyone, when we read a text. Empirical readers can read in many ways, and there is no law that tells them how to read, because they often use the text as a container for their own passions, which may come from outside the text or which the text may arouse by chance.

If you have ever happened to watch a comedy at a time of deep sadness, you will know that a funny movie is very difficult to enjoy at such a moment. That's not all: if you happen to see the same film again years later, you might still not be able to laugh, because every scene will remind you of the sadness you felt on the first occasion. Evidently, as an empirical spectator you would be "reading" the film in the wrong way. But "wrong" with respect to what? With respect to the type of spectators the director had in mind—that is, spectators inclined to smile and to follow a story which does not involve them personally. This type of spectator (or reader of a book) I call the model reader—a sort of ideal type whom the text not only foresees as a collaborator but also tries to create. If a text begins with "Once upon a time," it sends out a signal that immediately enables it to select its own model reader, who must be a child, or at least somebody willing to accept something that goes beyond the commonsensical and reasonable.

A childhood friend of mine, whom I hadn't seen for years, wrote to me after the publication of my second novel, *Foucault's Pendulum:* "Dear Umberto, I do not recall having told you the pathetic story of my uncle and aunt, but I think you were very indiscreet to use it in your novel." Well, in my book I recount a few episodes concerning an "Uncle Charles" and an "Aunt Catherine" who are the uncle and aunt of the protagonist, Jacopo Belpo, and it is true that these characters really did exist: with a few alterations, I tell a story from my childhood concerning an uncle and aunt—who had, however, different names. I wrote back to my friend saying that Uncle Charles and Aunt Catherine were my relations, not his, and that therefore I had the copyright; I was not even aware that he had had any uncles or aunts. My friend apologized: he had been so absorbed by the story that he thought he could recognize some incidents that had happened to his uncle and aunt—which is not impossible, because in wartime (which was the period to which my memories went back) similar things happen to different uncles and aunts.

What had happened to my friend? He had sought in the wood something that was instead in his private memory. It is right for me while walking in the wood to use every experience and every discovery to learn about life, about the past and the future. But since a wood is created for everybody, I must not look there for facts and sentiments which concern only myself. Otherwise (as

I have written in two recent books, *The Limits of Interpretation* and *Interpretation and Overinterpretation*),[10] I am not interpreting a text but rather *using* it. It is not at all forbidden to use a text for daydreaming, and we do this frequently, but daydreaming is not a public affair; it leads us to move within the narrative wood as if it were our own private garden.

One must therefore observe the rules of the game, and the model reader is someone eager to play such a game. My friend forgot the rules and superimposed his own expectations as empirical reader on the expectations that the author wanted from a model reader.

Certainly the author has, at his disposal, particular genre signals that he can use to give instructions to his model reader; but frequently these signals can be highly ambiguous. *Pinocchio*, by Carlo Collodi, begins with the following passage:

> Once upon a time there was . . . A King!, my little readers will at once say. No, children, you're wrong. Once upon a time there was a piece of wood.

It is a very complex beginning. At first, Collodi seems to indicate that a fairy tale is about to start. As soon as his readers are convinced that it is a story for children, children appear on the scene as the author's interlocutors and then, reasoning like children who are used to fairy tales, make a wrong prediction. So perhaps the story is not meant for children? But to correct this erroneous prediction, the author then turns to his young readers again, so they can continue to read the story as if it were for them and simply assume that it is a tale not about a king but about a puppet. And in the end they will not be disappointed. Yet that beginning is a wink to adult readers. Mightn't the fairy tale also be for them? And mightn't the wink indicate that they should read it in a different light, yet at the same time pretend to be children in order to understand the allegorical meanings of the tale? Such a beginning was enough to inspire a whole series of psychoanalytical, anthropological, and satirical readings of *Pinocchio,* not all of which are preposterous. Perhaps Collodi wanted to play a *double jeu,* and much of the fascination of this little, big book derives from this suspicion.

Who lays down these rules of the game and these limitations? In other words, who is it that constructs the model reader? "The author," my little listeners will immediately say.

But after making the distinction between the model reader and the empirical one with such difficulty, should we think of the author as an empirical entity who writes the story and decides which model reader he or she should construct, for reasons that perhaps cannot be confessed and are known only to his or her psychoanalyst? I'll tell you at once that I couldn't really care less about the empirical author of a narrative text (or, indeed, of any text). I know that I shall offend many members of my audience who perhaps spend much of their time reading biographies of Jane Austen or Proust, Dostoyevski or Salinger, and I realize only too well how wonderful and thrilling it is to peek into the private lives of real people whom we have come to love as close friends. It was a great example and comfort to me to learn in my impatient youth as a scholar that Kant had written his philosophical masterpiece at the venerable age of fifty-seven; likewise, I have always been terribly jealous when I remembered that Raymond Radiguet wrote *Le Diable au corps* at the age of twenty.

But this knowledge does not help us decide whether Kant was right in increasing the number of categories from ten to twelve, or whether *Le Diable au corps* is a masterpiece (it would still have been so even if Radiguet had written it at the age of fifty-seven). The possible hermaphroditism of the Mona Lisa is an interesting aesthetic subject, whereas the sexual habits of Leonardo da Vinci are, so far as my "reading" of that painting is concerned, mere gossip.

In my subsequent lectures, I shall often refer to one of the greatest books ever written, Gérard de Nerval's *Sylvie.* I read it at the age of twenty and still keep rereading it. When I was young

I wrote a very poor paper about it, and beginning in 1976 I held a series of seminars about it at the University of Bologna, the result being three doctoral dissertations and a special issue of the journal *VS* in 1982.[11] In 1984, at Columbia University, I devoted a graduate course to *Sylvie,* and some very interesting term papers were written about it. By now I know every comma and every secret mechanism of that novella. This experience of rereading a text over the course of forty years has shown me how silly those people are who say that dissecting a text and engaging in meticulous close reading is the death of its magic. Every time I pick up *Sylvie,* even though I know it in such an anatomical way—perhaps *because* I know it so well—I fall in love with it again, as if I were reading it for the first time.

Here is the beginning of *Sylvie,* followed by two English translations:

Je sortais d'un théâtre où tous les soirs je paraissais aux avant-scènes en grande tenue de soupirant . . .

1. I came out of a theater, where I appeared every evening in the full dress of a sighing lover.

2. I came out of a theater, where I used to spend every evening in the proscenium boxes in the role of an ardent wooer.[12]

The imperfect tense does not exist in English, so a translator can choose among various ways of rendering the French imperfect. The imperfect is a very interesting tense because it is both durative and iterative. As a durative, it tells us that something was happening in the past but does not give us any precise time, and the beginning and the end of the action are unknown. As an iterative, it implies that the action has been repeated. But one is never certain when it is iterative, when it is durative, or when it is both. At the start of *Sylvie,* for example, the first "sortais" is durative, because leaving a theater is an action which requires a certain lapse of time. But the second imperfect, "paraissais," is both durative and iterative. It is clear from the text that the character went to that theater every evening, but the use of the imperfect would suggest that this was the case even without this clarification. It is the ambiguity of this tense that makes it the most suitable for recounting dreams or nightmares. It is also the one used in fairy tales. "Once upon a time" is "C'era una volta" in Italian: "una volta" can be translated by "once," but the imperfect tense hints at a time which was uncertain, perhaps cyclical, rendered in English by "upon a time."

In rendering the iterative meaning of the French "paraissais," the first translation merely relies on the expression "every evening," whereas the second emphasizes the frequentative aspect with the phrase "I used to." This is not just a series of trivial incidents: much of the enjoyment in reading *Sylvie* arises from a well-calculated alternation between the imperfect and the simple past, the use of the imperfect creating a dreamlike atmosphere in the story, as if we were looking at something through half-closed eyes. Nerval did not think of an anglophone model reader, because English was too precise for his aims.

I shall return to Nerval's use of the imperfect in my next lecture, but we shall see in a while how important this tense is for our discussion of the author and of his or her voice. Let us now consider the "Je" with which the story begins. Books written in the first person may lead the naive reader to think that the "I" in the text is the author. It isn't, of course; it's the narrator, the voice that narrates. P. G. Wodehouse once wrote the memoirs of a dog in the first person—a matchless illustration of the fact that the narrative voice is not necessarily that of the author.

In *Sylvie* we must deal with three entities. The first is a gentleman who was born in 1808 and died (by committing suicide) in 1855—and who, by the way, was not even called Gérard de Nerval; his real name was Gérard Labrunie. With Michelin guide in hand, many visitors to Paris still look for the rue de la Vieille Lanterne, where he hanged himself. Some of them have never understood *Sylvie*'s beauty.

The second entity is the man who says "I" in the novella. This character is not Gérard Labrunie. All we know about him is that he tells us the story and does not kill himself at the end, when he offers the melancholy reflection: "Illusions fall like the husk of a fruit, one after another, and the fruit is experience."

My students and I decided to call him *Je-rard,* but since English cannot render this pun, we shall call him the narrator. The narrator is not Mr. Labrunie, for the same reason that the person who begins *Gulliver's Travels* saying, "My Father had a small Estate in Nottinghamshire; I was the Third of five Sons. He sent me to Emanuel-College in Cambridge, at Fourteen Years old," is not Jonathan Swift, who had studied at Trinity College in Dublin. The model reader is asked to be moved by the narrator's lost illusions, not by those of Mr. Labrunie.

Finally, there is a third entity, whom it is usually difficult to identify and whom I call the model author, to create symmetry with the model reader. Labrunie may have been a plagiarist and *Sylvie* might have been written by the grandfather of Fernando Pessoa, but the model author of *Sylvie* is the anonymous "voice" that starts the story with "Je sortais d'un théâtre" and ends by having Sylvie say "Pauvre Adrienne! elle est morte au couvent de Saint-S..., vers 1832." We know nothing else about him, or rather we know only what this voice says between the first and last chapters of the story. The last chapter is called "Dernier feuillet," or "The Last Leaf": beyond that, the only thing left is the narrative wood, and it is up to us to enter and go through it. Once we have accepted this rule of the game, we can even take the liberty of giving this voice a name, a nom de plume. With your permission, I think I have found a very beautiful one: Nerval. Nerval is neither Labrunie nor the narrator. Nerval is not a *he,* just as George Eliot is not a *she* (only Mary Ann Evans was). Nerval would be *Es* in German, and in English can be *It* (unfortunately, Italian grammar would force me to give it a gender).

We could say that this It—who at the beginning of the story is not yet evident, or perhaps is present only as a series of faint traces—at the end of our reading will be identified with what every aesthetic theory calls "style." Yes, of course, at the end the model author can be recognized also as a style, and this style will be so clear and unmistakable that we will see it is undoubtedly the same voice that begins the novel *Aurélia* by saying "Le rêve est une seconde vie"—"Dream is a second life."

But the term "style" says too much and too little. It makes us think that the model author (to quote Stephen Dedalus), isolated in his perfection, "like the God of creation, remains within or behind or beyond or above his handiwork, invisible, refined, out of existence, paring his fingernails."[13] The model author, on the other hand, is a voice that speaks to us affectionately (or imperiously, or slyly), that wants us beside it. This voice is manifested as a narrative strategy, as a set of instructions which is given to us step by step and which we have to follow when we decide to act as the model reader.

In the vast range of works on the theory of narrative, on the aesthetics of reception, and on reader-oriented criticism, there are various entities called Ideal Readers, Implied Readers, Virtual Readers, Metareaders, and so on—each of them evoking as their own counterpart an Ideal or Implied or Virtual Author.[14] These terms are not always synonymous. My Model Reader is, for instance, very similar to the Implied Reader of Wolfgang Iser. Nevertheless, for Iser the reader "actually causes the text to reveal its potential multiplicity of connections. These connections are the product of the reader's mind working on the raw material of the text, though they are not the text itself—for this consists just of sentences, statements, information, etc. . . . This interplay obviously does not take place in the text itself, but can only come into being through the process of reading . . . This process formulates something that is unformulated in the text and yet represents its 'intention.'"[15]

Such a process is more similar to the one I outlined in 1962 in my book *Opera Aperta (The Open Work).*[16] The model reader I proposed later is, on the contrary, a set of textual instructions, displayed by the text's linear manifestation precisely as a set of sentences or other signals. As Paola Pugliatti has remarked,

> Iser's phenomenological perspective assigns to the reader a privilege that has been considered the prerogative of texts: namely, that of establishing a "point of view," thereby determining the text's meaning. Eco's Model Reader (1979) not only figures as the text's interactant and cooperator; much more—and, in a sense, less—he/she is born with it, being the sinews of its interpretive strategy. Thus the competence of Model Readers is determined by the kind of genetic imprinting that the text has transmitted to them . . . Created with—and imprisoned in—the text, they enjoy as much freedom as the text is willing to grant them.[17]

It is true that in *The Act of Reading* Iser says that "the concept of implied reader is therefore a textual structure anticipating the presence of a recipient"; but he adds, "without necessarily defining him." For Iser, "the reader's role is not identical with the fictitious reader portrayed in the text. The latter is merely one component of the reader's role."[18]

In the course of my lectures, even though I acknowledge the existence of all the other components so brilliantly studied by Iser, I shall basically focus my attention on that "fictitious reader" portrayed in the text, assuming that the main business of interpretation is to figure out the nature of this reader, in spite of its ghostly existence. If you wish, you may say that I am more "German" than Iser, more abstract, or—as noncontinental philosophers would say—more speculative.

In this sense I would speak of model readers not only for texts that are open to multiple points of view but also for those that foresee a very obedient reader. In other words, there is a model reader not only for *Finnegans Wake* but also for a railway timetable, and the texts expect a different kind of cooperation from each of them. Obviously, we are more excited by Joyce's instructions for "an ideal reader affected by an ideal insomnia," but we should also pay attention to the set of reading instructions provided by the timetable.

In the same vein, my model author is not necessarily a glorious voice, a sublime strategy: the model author acts and reveals himself even in the most squalid pornographic novel, to tell us that the descriptions we are given must be a stimulus for our imagination and for our physical reactions. As an example of a model author who shamelessly reveals himself to readers from the very first page, giving them orders about the emotions they are supposed to feel even if the book does not manage to communicate them, let's look at the beginning of *My Gun Is Quick*, by Mickey Spillane:

> When you sit at home comfortably folded up in a chair beside a fire, have you ever thought what goes on outside there? Probably not. You pick a book and read about things and stuff, getting a vicarious kick from people and events that never happened ... . Fun, isn't it? ... Even the old Romans did it, spiced their life with actions when they sat in the Coliseum and watched wild animals rip a bunch of humans apart, reveling in the sight of blood and terror ... Oh, it's great to watch, all right. Life through a keyhole ... But remember this: there *are* things happening out there ... There isn't a Coliseum any more, but the city is a bigger bowl, and it seats more people. The razor-sharp claws aren't those of wild animals, but man's can be just as sharp and twice as vicious. You have to be quick, and you have to be able, or you become one of the devoured ... You have to be quick. And able. Or you'll be dead.[19]

Here the presence of the model author is explicit and, as I have said, shameless. There are other cases in which, with greater effrontery but more subtlety, model author, empirical author, narrator, and even vaguer entities are shown, are staged in the narrative text with the explicit aim of confusing the reader. Let us go back to Poe's *Arthur Gordon Pym*. Two installments of those adventures were published in 1837, in the *Southern Literary Mes-*

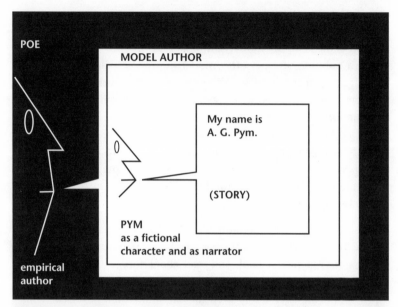

Figure 1

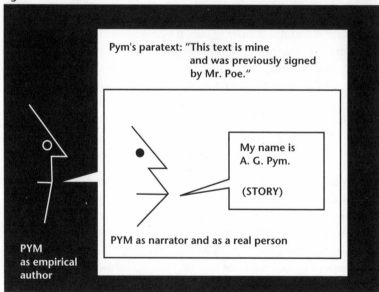

Figure 2

senger, more or less in the form that we now read them. The text began with "My name is Arthur Gordon Pym" and thus presented a first-person narrator, but that text appeared with the name of Poe as the empirical author (see Figure 1). In 1838 the whole story was published in book form, but without the author's name on the title page. Instead, there was a preface signed "A. G. Pym" presenting the adventures as facts, and telling readers that in the *Southern Literary Messenger* "the name of Mr. Poe was affixed to the articles" because nobody would have believed the story, so it was just as well to present it "under the garb of fiction."

So we have a Mr. Pym, allegedly an empirical author, who is also the narrator of a true story, and who moreover has written a preface which is part not of the narrative text but of the *paratext.*[20] Mr. Poe fades into the background, becoming a sort of character of the paratext (see Figure 2). But at the end of the story, just when it is interrupted, a note is added explaining how the final chapters have been lost owing to the "late sudden and distressing death of Mr. Pym," a death which is supposed to be "well known to the public through the medium of the daily press." This note, which is unsigned (and which has certainly not been written by Mr. Pym, whose death it speaks of), cannot be attributed to Poe, because it talks about Mr. Poe's being the first editor, even accusing him of not having known how to grasp the cryptographic nature of the figures Pym had included in the text. At this point the reader is led to believe that Pym is a fictitious character who speaks not only as the narrator but also at the beginning of the preface, which thus becomes part of the story and not of the paratext. The text is certainly the product of a third, anonymous, empirical author—who is the author of the note (a real paratext), in which he speaks of Poe in the same terms as Pym did in his false paratext; so that the reader now wonders whether Mr. Poe is a real person or a character in two different stories, the one told by Pym's false paratext and the other told by Mr. X's true but mendacious paratext (see Figure 3). As a last conundrum, this mysterious Mr. Pym begins his story with "My name is Arthur Gordon Pym"—an incipit which not only anticipates Melville's "Call me Ishmael" (a connection which is of little significance) but also seems to parody a text in which Poe, before writing *Pym,* had parodied a certain Morris Mattson, who had started one of his novels with "My name is Paul Ulric."[21]

Readers would be justified if they started to suspect that the empirical author was Poe, who invented a fictitious real person, Mr. X, who speaks of a false real person, Mr. Pym, who in his turn acts as the narrator of a fictional story. The only embarrassing thing is that these fictitious persons speak of the real Mr. Poe as if he were an inhabitant of their fictitious universe (see Figure 4).

Who is the model author in all this textual tangle? Whoever it is, it is the voice, or the strategy, which confounds the various presumed empirical authors, so that the model reader can't help becoming enmeshed in such a catoptric trick.

Let's go back to rereading *Sylvie.* By using an imperfect tense at the beginning, the voice which we have decided to call Nerval tells us that we are to prepare ourselves for listening to a reminiscence. After four pages the voice immediately shifts from the imperfect to the simple past and recounts a night spent in the club after the theater. We are to understand that here, too, we are listening to one of the narrator's reminiscences, but that he is now recalling a precise moment. It is the moment in which, while talking to a friend about the actress he has loved for some time, without ever approaching her, he realizes that what he loves is not a woman but an image ("I pursue an image, nothing more"). Now, however, in the reality fixed precisely by the past tense, he reads in a newspaper that, in reality, that very evening in Loisy, where he spent his childhood, they are holding the traditional festival of archers, which he used to take part in as a boy, when he was infatuated with the beautiful Sylvie.

In the second chapter, the story returns to the imperfect. The narrator spends a few hours in a half-sleep in which he recalls a similar festival, presumably when he was a boy. He remembers

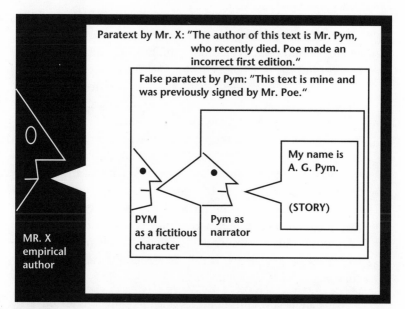

Figure 3

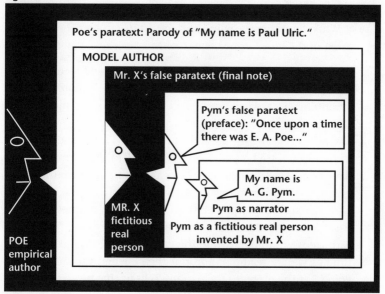

Figure 4

gentle Sylvie, who loved him, and the beautiful, haughty Adrienne, who had sung that evening on the lawn; she had been an almost miraculous apparition, and had then disappeared forever behind the walls of a convent. Between sleeping and waking, the narrator wonders whether he still hopelessly loves the same image—that is, whether in some inexplicable way both Adrienne and the actress are the same woman.

In the third chapter the narrator is seized by the desire to return to the scene of his childhood memories, calculates that he could arrive there before dawn, goes out, takes a carriage, and, during the journey, as he is beginning to make out the roads, hills, and villages of his childhood, begins a new reminiscence— this one more recent, only about three years before the time of his journey. But the reader is introduced to this new stream of memories by a sentence which, if we read it carefully, seems amazing:

Pendant que la voiture monte les côtes, recomposons les souvenirs du temps où j'y venais si souvent.

While the carriage climbs the slope, let us recollect the memories of the time I came there so often.

Who is it who pronounces (or writes) this sentence and calls for our involvement? The narrator? But the narrator, who is describing a carriage ride made years before the moment in which he is narrating, should say something like, "While the carriage was going up the hills, I recollected [or "I started recollecting," or "I told myself 'let us recollect'"] the memories of the days when I used to go there so often." Who is—or rather, who are—those "we" who together have to bring back the memories and therefore make preparations for another journey into the past? Who are the "we" who have to do it now, "while the carriage is climbing" (while the carriage is moving at the same time as we are reading), and not then, "when the carriage was going," at the moment the narrator tells us that he was recollect-

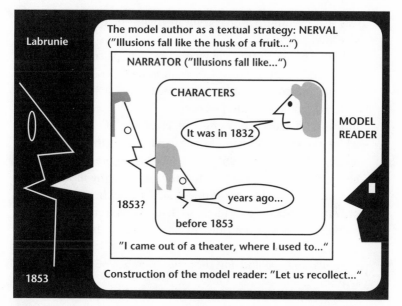

Figure 5

ing? This is not the voice of the narrator; it is the voice of Nerval, the model author, who for a moment speaks in the first person in the story and says to us model readers: "While the narrator is going up the hills in his carriage, let us recompose (with him, of course, but you and I, too) the memories of the time when he would come so often to these places." This is not a monologue but one part of a dialogue among three parties: Nerval, who surreptitiously enters the narrator's discourse; we, who have been called upon to participate just as surreptitiously, when we thought we could observe the event from the outside (we, who thought we had never left a theater); and the narrator, who is not excluded, since it was he who came to those places so often ("J'y venais si souvent," "I used to go there so often").

It should also be pointed out that many pages could be written about that "j'y." Does it mean "there," there where the narrator was that evening? Or does it mean "here," here where Nerval is suddenly taking us?

At this point, in this tale where time and place are so inextricably tangled, even the voices seem to be confounded. But this confusion is so admirably orchestrated that it is imperceptible—or almost, since we are perceiving it. It is not confusion but a moment of clearsightedness, an epiphany of storytelling, in which the three components of the narrative trinity—the model author, the narrator, and the reader—all appear together (see Figure 5). They must appear together because the model author and the model reader are entities that become clear to each other only in the process of reading, so that each one creates the other. I think this is true not only for narrative texts but for any sort of text.

In his *Philosophical Investigations* (number 66), Wittgenstein writes:

> Consider for example the proceedings that we call "games": I mean board-games, card-games, ball-games, Olympic games, and so on. What is common to them all?—Don't say: "There must be something common, or they would not be called 'games'"—but look and see whether there is anything common to all.—For if you look at them you will not see something that is common to all, but similarities, relationships, and a whole series of them at that.[22]

The personal pronouns in this passage do not indicate an empirical character or an empirical reader; they are merely textual strategies, set out as a form of appeal, as in the beginning of a dialogue. The intervention of a speaking subject occurs simultaneously with the creation of a model reader who knows how to continue the game of inquiry into the nature of games; and the intellectual disposition of this reader (even the urge to play on the subject of playing games) is determined only by the type of interpretive moves that that voice asks him or her to make: to look, to see, to consider, to find relationships and similarities. In the same way, the author is but a textual strategy that is capable of establishing semantic correlations and that asks to be imitated: when this voice says "I mean," it is inviting us to come to an agreement, so that the word "game" should be taken as referring to board games, card games, and so on. But this voice does not define the word "game"; rather, it asks *us* to define it, or to recognize that it can be defined satisfactorily only in terms of "family resemblances." In this text, Wittgenstein is merely a philosophical style, and his model reader merely the will and ability to adapt to this style, cooperating to make it possible.

So I, a voice without body or sex or any history—unless it be the voice which starts with this first lecture and will end with the last—invite you, gentle readers, to play my game with me during our next five meetings.

THE WOODS
OF LOISY

There are two ways of walking through a wood. The first is to try one or several routes (so as to get out of the wood as fast as possible, say, or to reach the house of grandmother, Tom Thumb, or Hansel and Gretel); the second is to walk so as to discover what the wood is like and find out why some paths are accessible and others are not. Similarly, there are two ways of going through a narrative text. Any such text is addressed, above all, to a model reader of the first level, who wants to know, quite rightly, how the story ends (whether Ahab will manage to capture the whale, or whether Leopold Bloom will meet Stephen Dedalus after coming across him a few times on the sixteenth of June 1904). But every text is also addressed to a model reader of the second level, who wonders what sort of reader that story would like him or her to become and who wants to discover precisely how the model author goes about serving as a guide for the reader. In order to know how a story ends, it is usually enough to read it once. In contrast, to identify the model author the text has to be read many times, and certain stories endlessly. Only when empirical readers have discovered the model author, and have understood (or merely begun to understand) what it wanted from them, will they become full-fledged model readers.

Perhaps the text in which the voice of the model author appeals most explicitly for the second-level reader's collaboration is a famous detective story: *The Murder of Roger Ackroyd,* by Agatha Christie. Everyone knows the story. A narrator, speaking in the first person, tells how Hercule Poirot gradually comes to discover the culprit, except that at the end we learn from Poirot that the culprit is the narrator, who cannot deny his guilt. But while he is waiting to be arrested and about to commit suicide, the narrator turns directly to his readers. Indeed, this narrator is an ambiguous figure because not only is he the character who says "I" in a book written by somebody else; he also appears as the man who has physically written what we are reading (like Arthur Gordon Pym), and at the end of the story he acts as the model author of his own diary—or, if you prefer, the model author speaks through him, or, better, we enjoy through him the narrative representation of a model author.

The narrator, therefore, invites his readers to read the book again from the beginning because, he states, if they had been perceptive, they would have realized that he had never lied. At most he had been reticent, because a text is a lazy machine that expects a lot of collaboration from the reader. And he not only invites the reader to read it again but physically helps the second-level reader to do so by quoting at the end some of the sentences from the opening chapters.

> I am rather pleased with myself as a writer. What could be neater, for instance, than the following: "The letters were brought in at twenty minutes to nine. It was just on ten minutes to nine when I left him, the letter still unread. I hesitated with my hand on the door handle, looking back and wondering if there was anything I had left undone." All true, you see. But suppose I had put a row of stars after the first sentence? Would somebody then have wondered what exactly happened in that blank ten minutes?

At this point the narrator explains what he really did in those ten minutes. Then he continues:

> I must admit that it gave me rather a shock to run into Parker just outside the door. I have faithfully recorded that fact. Then later, when the body was discovered, and I had sent Parker to

telephone for the police, what a judicious use of words: "I did what little had to be done"! It was quite a little—just to shove the dictaphone into my bag and push back the chair against the wall, in its proper place.[1]

Of course model authors are not always so explicit. If we go back to *Sylvie*, for example, we find ourselves dealing with an author who perhaps didn't want us to read the text again, or rather who wanted us to reread but did not want us to understand what had happened to us while reading it the first time. Indeed Proust, in the pages he dedicated to Nerval, describes the impressions that any of us would be likely to have after reading *Sylvie* for the first time:

> What we have here is one of those rainbow-painted pictures, never to be seen in real life, or even called up by words, but sometimes brought before us in a dream or called up by music. Sometimes, in the moment of falling asleep, we see them, and try to seize and define them. Then we wake up and they are gone . . . It is something vague and haunting, like a memory. It is atmospheric, the atmosphere of Sylvie, a colouring in the air like the bloom on a grape . . . But it is not in the words, it is not said, it is all among the words, like the morning mist at Chantilly.[2]

The word "mist" is very important. *Sylvie* really does seem to affect its readers like a mist, as if we were looking at a landscape through half-closed eyes, without clearly distinguishing the shape of things. But it is not that the things cannot be distinguished; on the contrary, the descriptions of landscapes and people in *Sylvie* are very clear and precise, even of a neoclassical clarity. What in fact readers cannot grasp is where they are in time. As Georges Poulet said, Nerval's past "plays ring-around-the-rosy with him."[3]

The fundamental mechanism in *Sylvie* is based on a continual alternation between flashbacks and flashforwards, and on certain groups of embedded flashbacks.

When we are told a story which refers to a narrative time 1 (the time at which the narrated events occur, which may be two hours ago or a thousand years ago), both the narrator (in the first or third person) and the characters can refer to something that happened prior to the time of the narrated events. Or they can hint at something that, at the time of these events, has yet to occur and that is anticipated. As Gérard Genette says, a flashback seems to make up for something the author has forgotten, whereas the flashforward is a manifestation of narrative impatience.[4]

Everyone uses such techniques when describing past events: "Hey, listen to this! Yesterday I met John—perhaps you remember, he's the one who used to go jogging every morning two years ago [*flashback*]. Well, he was very pale, and I must admit I only realized later why [*flashforward*]—oh! I forgot to tell you that when I saw him he was coming out of a bar, and it was only ten o'clock in the morning, get it? [*flashback*]—anyway, John tells me that—Oh, God, you'll never guess what he told me [*flashforward*] . . ." I hope *I* won't be so confusing in the rest of this discussion. But, with greater artistic sense, Nerval certainly confounds us throughout *Sylvie* with a dizzying game of flashbacks and flashforwards.

The narrator of the story is in love with an actress, without knowing whether his love is reciprocated. An item in the newspaper suddenly brings back memories of his childhood. He returns home, and in a half-sleeping, half-waking state he remembers two girls, Sylvie and Adrienne. Adrienne was like a vision: blonde, beautiful, tall, and slender. She was "a mirage of glory and beauty"; "the blood of the Valois flowed in her veins." Sylvie, in contrast, looked like a "petite fille" from the neighboring village, a country girl with dark eyes and "slightly tanned skin," childishly jealous of the attention the narrator paid to Adrienne.

After a few sleepless hours, the narrator decides to take a carriage and return to the place of his memories. During the journey he begins to recall other events ("recomposons les souvenirs . . .")—events that occurred in a past closer to the time of the journey: "quelques années s'étaient écoulées" ("some years had passed"). In this long flashback, Adrienne appears only fleetingly and as a memory within a memory, while Sylvie is strikingly alive and real. She is no longer a "little village girl . . . She had become so beautiful!" Her figure is lithe; she has something Athenian in her smile. She is now endowed with all the graces that the narrator in his youth attributed to Adrienne, and perhaps the narrator can satisfy his need for love with her. They pay a visit to Sylvie's aunt, and, in a moving scene that seems to foretell their possible happiness, they dress up as fiancés from an earlier era. But it is too late, or too soon. The narrator returns to Paris the following day.

Here he is now, as the carriage climbs a hill, bringing him back to his native village. It is four o'clock in the morning, and the narrator starts a new flashback, which we shall return to in another lecture—and please appreciate my flashforward, because here (in Chapter 7) the times really get completely mixed up and it is impossible to determine whether the last fleeting glimpse he had of Adrienne, which he only now remembers, was before or after the party he has just recalled. But the parenthesis is brief. We meet the narrator again on his arrival at Loisy, when an archery contest is drawing to a close, and he finds Sylvie once more. She is now a fascinating young woman, and the narrator recalls with her various aspects of their childhood and adolescence (the flashbacks occur in the story almost unnoticed); but he realizes that she, too, has changed. She has become a craftswoman, producing gloves; she reads Rousseau, can sing arias from opera, has even learned "phrasing." And finally, she is about to marry the narrator's foster-brother and boyhood friend. The narrator realizes that the age of illusion cannot be recaptured and that he has lost his last chance.

Back in Paris, the narrator finally succeeds in having a love affair with Aurélie, the actress. At this point the story speeds up:

the narrator lives with the actress, understands that he doesn't really love her, and returns with her a few times to the village, where Sylvie is now a happy mother; she is a friend and perhaps a sister to him. In the final chapter, the narrator, after being abandoned by the actress (or letting himself be abandoned), speaks once more to Sylvie, reflecting on his lost illusions.

The story could be very banal, but the tangle of flashbacks and flashforwards makes it magically unreal. As Proust said, "One is constantly obliged to turn back to an earlier page to see where one is, if it is the present or the past recalled."[5] The misty effect is so pervasive that the reader usually fails in this task. It is clear why Proust, who was fascinated with the search for things past and who would end his work under the banner of time recaptured, considered Nerval both a master and an unsuccessful forerunner who lost his battle with time.

But who is it who loses the battle? Gérard Labrunie, empirical author, destined to commit suicide? Nerval, model author? Or the reader? While he was writing *Sylvie,* Labrunie stayed several times in a clinic, in a rather critical state of mental health, and in *Aurélia* he tells us that he wrote laboriously, "almost always in pencil, on scattered bits of paper, following the haphazard course of my daydreams or my walks." He wrote as an empirical reader at first reads, without seeing temporal ties, the before and after. Proust will say that *Sylvie* "is a dream of a dream," but Labrunie really did write as if he were dreaming. This is not true of Nerval as model author. The apparent uncertainty concerning times and places which constitutes the fascination of *Sylvie* (and brings about a crisis in the first-level reader) is founded on a narrative strategy and grammatical tactics as perfect as clockwork—which, however, are visible only to the second-level reader.

How does a person become a second-level model reader? We must reconstruct the sequence of events that the narrator virtually lost, in order to understand not so much how the narrator lost it but how Nerval leads the reader to lose it.

In order to understand what has to be done, we must refer to a fundamental theme of all modern narrative theories, the distinction that the Russian Formalists made between *fabula* and *sjužet*—terms that I shall translate in the commonly accepted way as *story* and *plot*.

The story of Ulysses, both as told by Homer and as reformulated by James Joyce, was probably known to the Greeks before the *Odyssey* was written. Ulysses leaves burning Troy and, with his companions, gets lost at sea. He meets strange peoples and horrible monsters—Laestrygonians, Polyphemus, the Lotus Eaters, Scylla and Charybdis; he descends to the underworld, escapes from the Sirens, and finally is captured by the nymph Calypso. At this point the gods decide to help him return to his homeland. Calypso is forced to liberate Ulysses, who returns to the sea, is shipwrecked, and tells Alcinoüs his tale. Then he sets sail for Ithaca, where he defeats the suitors of Penelope and is reunited with her. The story proceeds in a linear fashion from an initial moment, T_1, toward a final moment, T_x (see Figure 6).

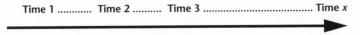

Time 1 .... Time 2 .... Time 3 .... Time x

Figure 6: Story

The plot of the *Odyssey,* however, is quite different. The *Odyssey* begins *in medias res,* at a moment T_0, when the voice that we call Homer begins to speak. We can identify this moment, as we please, either with the day on which Homer allegedly began to narrate or with the moment we begin to read. What matters is that the plot starts at a moment T_1, when Ulysses is already Calypso's prisoner. Between this moment and a moment T_2, which corresponds to Book 8, Ulysses escapes from Calypso's amorous advances, is shipwrecked among the Phaeacians, and tells his tale. But at this point the story goes backward to a time that we shall call T_{-3} and deals with Ulysses' previous adventures. This flashback lasts for a large part of the epic, and only in Book

13 does the text bring us back to where we were in Book 8. Ulysses concludes his reminiscences and sets sail for Ithaca (see Figure 7).

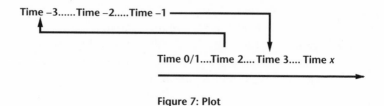

Figure 7: Plot

There are some tales, such as fairy tales, which are called "simple forms" because they have only a story, without any plot. "Little Red Riding Hood" is one of these. It begins with the little girl's leaving home and entering the wood, and ends with the death of the wolf and the girl's return home. Another example of simple form may be Edward Lear's limericks:

> There was an old man of Peru
> who watched his wife making a stew;
> But once by mistake
> In a stove she did bake
> That unfortunate man of Peru.

Let's try to tell this story as it might be reported by the *New York Times*: "Lima, March 17. Yesterday Alvaro Gonzales Barreto (41, two children, accountant at Chemical Bank of Peru) was erroneously cooked in a shepherd's pie by his wife, Lolita Sanchez de Medinaceli . . ." Why is this story not as good as Lear's? Because Lear tells a story, but the story is the content of his tale. This content has a form, an organization, which is that of the simple form, and Lear does not complicate it with a plot. Instead, he expresses the form of his narrative content through a form of expression, consisting of the metrical patterns and playful rhymes typical of the limerick. The story is communicated through a narrative discourse (see Figure 8).[6]

We could say that story and plot are not functions of language but structures that can nearly always be translated into another semiotic system. In fact I can recount the same story of the *Odyssey,* organized according to the same plot, by means of linguistic paraphrase, as I have just done, or in a film or comic

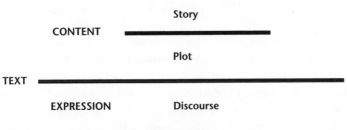

Figure 8: Text

book, since there are flashback signals in these two semiotic systems as well. On the other hand, the words with which Homer tells the story are part of the Homeric text and cannot be paraphrased or translated into images very easily.

A narrative text may conceivably lack a plot, but it cannot possibly do without story or discourse. Even the story of Little Red Riding Hood has come down to us through different discourses—Grimm's, Perrault's, our mother's. Discourse is also part of a model author's strategy. Lear's indirect pathetic comment telling us that the old man of Peru was "unfortunate" is an element of discourse, not of story. In a certain sense, it is discourse, not story, that lets the model reader know whether he should be touched by the old man's fate. The very form of the limerick, which cues us to view the content as absurd, ironic, and tongue-in-cheek, is also part of discourse, so that in choosing this form Lear is telling us that we can laugh at a story which might make us cry if told in the discursive mode of the *New York Times*.

When the text of *Sylvie* says "While the carriage is going up the hills, let us recollect the memories of the days I went there so often," we know that it is not the narrator but the model author who is speaking to us. It is clear that at this moment the model author reveals Itself in the way It organizes the story: not by means of a plot, but through a narrative discourse.

Many theories of literature have insisted that the voice of the model author should be heard solely through the organization of facts (story and plot); such theories reduce the presence of discourse to a minimum—not as if it were not there, but as if the reader should not be aware of its indications. For T. S. Eliot, "the only way of expressing emotion in the form of art is by finding an 'objective correlative'; in other words a set of objects, a situation, a chain of events which shall be the formula of that particular emotion."[7] Proust, although he praises the style of Flaubert, nevertheless faults him for writing phrases such as "those good old inns which always have something country-like about them." He quotes the line "Madame Bovary approached the fireplace" and observes with satisfaction, "It was never said that she was cold." Proust wants "a tightly knit style, of porphyry, without any cracks, without any additions," in which we see a mere "apparition" of things.[8]

A term like "apparition" reminds us of the "epiphany" of Joyce. In *The Dubliners,* there are some epiphanies in which the mere representation of events tells readers what they must try to understand. On the other hand, in the epiphany of the girl-bird in *A Portrait of the Artist as a Young Man,* it is the discourse, not the simple story, that orients the reader. This is why I think it is impossible to translate the apparition of the girl in *A Portrait* into a film, whereas John Huston managed to render the atmosphere of a story such as "The Dead" (in his film of the same name) by simply dramatizing the facts, the situations, and people's conversations.

I have been obliged to make this long digression on the various levels of the narrative text because the time has come to answer a very tricky question: If there are texts that have only a story and no plot, isn't it also possible that some texts, like *Sylvie*, might have only a plot and no story? Is *Sylvie* simply a text that says how impossible it is to reconstruct a story? Does the text ask the reader to fall ill, like Labrunie—incapable of distinguishing dreams, memories, and reality? Doesn't the very use of the imperfect perhaps say that the author wanted us to get lost, not that we should analyze his use of the imperfect?

It is a matter of choosing between two statements. In one, Labrunie ironically says (in a letter to Alexandre Dumas which appears in *Les Filles du feu*) that his works are no more complicated than Hegel's metaphysics, adding that "they would lose their charm if they were explained, if that were possible." The other is certainly by Nerval and appears in the last chapter of *Sylvie:* "Such are the delusions [the French text says *chimères*] which charm and lead us astray in the morning of life. I have tried to set them down without too much order, but many hearts will understand me." Should we take Nerval to mean that he hasn't followed any order, or instead recognize that the order he has followed is not readily apparent? Should we assume that Proust—who analyzed in such detail Flaubert's use of verb tenses and who was so alert to the effects of narrative strategies—asked Nerval to do nothing more than seduce him with his imperfects, and thought that Nerval was using this cruel tense, which presents life as something ephemeral and passive, merely to inspire his readers with vague sadness? And is it likely that Labrunie could have taken such pains to order his work, yet did not want us to perceive and admire the devices he had used to cause us to lose our way?

I have been told that Coca-Cola tastes good because it contains some secret ingredients that the wizards in Atlanta will never reveal—but I do not like such Coke-oriented criticism. I am reluctant to think that Nerval would not have wanted the reader to recognize and appreciate his stylistic strategies. Nerval wanted us both to feel that the periods of time were blurred and to understand how he had managed to blend them.

One objection might be that my notion of literature does not correspond to Nerval's, and perhaps not even to Labrunie's; but let us return to the text of *Sylvie*. This story—which starts with a vague "Je sortais d'un théâtre," as if wanting to create an atmosphere similar to that of a fairy tale—ends with a date, the only one in the book. On the last page, when the narrator has lost all his illusions, Sylvie says, "Poor Adrienne! She died in the convent of Saint-S... around 1832."

Why should there be this imperious date which appears at the very end, the most strategic point of the text, and which seems to interrupt the spell with a precise reference? As Proust said, "One is constantly obliged to turn back to an earlier page to see where one is, if it is the present or the past recalled." And if we do go back, we realize that the whole narrative discourse is studded with temporal hints.

They are invisible on the first reading, but on the second they are quite obvious. At the time he tells his story, the narrator says that he has already been in love with the actress for a year. After the first flashback he refers to Adrienne as a "face forgotten for years," but he thinks about Sylvie and wonders, "Why have I forgotten her for three years?" At first the reader thinks that three years have passed since the first flashback, and gets even more lost, because if that were the case the narrator would be a mere boy instead of a pleasure-seeking young man. But at the beginning of the fourth chapter, at the start of the second flashback, when the carriage is going up the hill, the text opens with "Some years had passed." Since when? Probably from the childhood days that were described in the first flashback. The reader may think that some years had passed from the time of the first flashback to the time of the second, and that three years have elapsed from the time of the second until the time of the journey . . . During the second flashback, it is clear that the narrator stays in that place for one night and the following day. The seventh chapter (which has the most confused temporal sequence) begins with "It's four in the morning," and the following one tells us that the narrator arrives in Loisy toward dawn. From the moment the narrator returns to Paris and begins his love affair with the actress, indications of time become more frequent: we are told that "months passed"; after a particular event, "the following days" are mentioned; then we read of "two months later," then of "next summer," of "next day," "that evening," and so on. Perhaps this voice telling us of time links may want us to lose our sense of time, but it also encourages us to reconstruct the exact sequence of events.

That's why I would like you to look at the diagram shown in Figure 9. Please don't consider it a cruel, unnecessary exercise. It will help us grasp the mystery of *Sylvie* a little better. On the vertical axis, let's put the implicit chronological sequence of events (the story), which I have reconstructed, even where Nerval merely gives faint hints of it. On the horizontal axis, we have the sequence of chapters—that is, the plot. The sequence of the explicit story, which Nerval informs us about in the text, looks like a sawed-off, jagged horizontal line on the plot axis; from this line branch off vertical arrows pointing to the past. The continuous vertical arrows represent the narrator's flashbacks; the dotted ones stand for the flashbacks (hints, allusions, brief recollections) the narrator attributes to Sylvie or to other characters (including himself, when describing his memories to Aurélie). They should start from the virtual present perfect, in which the narrator is speaking, and point to a virtual past perfect. Both tenses, however, are continually disguised by the use of the imperfect.

At what moment does the narrator speak? That is to say, when is the T_0 at which he speaks? Since the text makes reference to the nineteenth century and since *Sylvie* was written in 1853, let's take 1853 as the Time Zero of the narration. This is a mere convention, a postulate on which to base my discussion. I could just as well have decided that the voice is speaking today, in

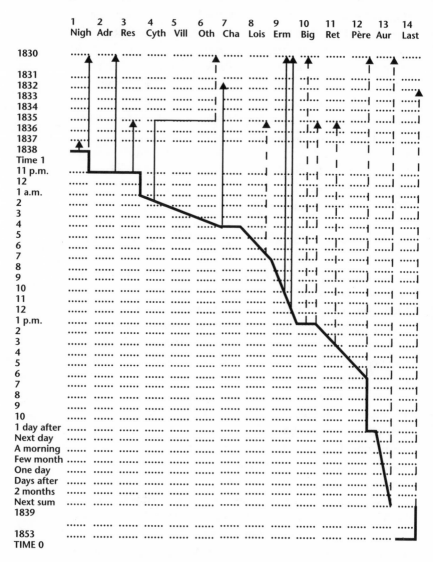

Figure 9

1993, while we are reading. What matters is that once a T_0 has been established, we can have an exact countdown, using only the data given by the narrative discourse.

If we calculate that Adrienne died in 1832, after the narrator had met her as a youth, and if we consider that, after the night he took the carriage and after he returned to Paris two days later, the narrator is fairly clear in telling us that months and not years have passed since he started his relationship with the actress, it is possible to establish, approximately, that the evening spoken about in the first three chapters and the whole episode of his return to Loisy occur in 1838. If we imagine the narrator at that time as a dandy in his early twenties, and if we take into account that the first flashback describes him as a boy of perhaps twelve years of age, we can establish that the first recollection goes back to 1830. And since we are told that as of 1838 three years had passed since the time referred to in the second flashback, we can assume that the events had taken place in about 1835. The final date, 1832, when the death of Adrienne occurs, is of help to us because in our reconstructed year 1835 Sylvie makes vague allusions leading us to think that at that time Adrienne was already dead ("Votre religieuse . . . Cela a mal tourné"—that is, "It had an unhappy ending," "It turned out badly"). Thus, having fixed two conventionally precise chronological references—1853 as Time Zero of the narrating voice, and an evening in 1838 as Time 1, in which the game of memories begins—we can establish a regressive series of times leading us back to 1830, as well as a progressive one, which leads to the final separation from the actress, more or less in 1839.

What does one gain from this reconstruction? Nothing at all, if one is only a first-level reader. One might, perhaps, be able to clear some of the mist, but loses the spell of being lost. Second-level readers, on the other hand, realize that these recollections do have an order and that these sudden shifts in time and quick returns to the historical present follow a rhythm. Nerval has managed to create his misty effects by composing a sort of musical score.

It is like a melody, which the reader can enjoy first for the effects it elicits, and later by discovering how an unexpected series of intervals can produce these effects. This score tells us how a tempo is imposed on the reader by "shifting gears," so to speak. Most of the flashbacks occur in the first twelve chapters, which cover twenty-four hours (from eleven o'clock at night, when the narrator leaves the theater, to the following evening, when he leaves his friends to return to Paris the next day). One could say that in these twenty-four hours, eight previous years are embedded. But this depends on an "optical" illusion resulting from my reconstruction. On the vertical axis of Figure 9,, I have scored all the steps of the story that *Sylvie* as a text *presupposes* but does not explicitly tell—because the narrator is unable to control these temporal strategies. Of these eight years, only a few points, a few scattered fragments, are retrieved. Thus, we have an enormously dilated space in the plot in which to narrate a few disconnected hours of the story, since these eight years are not narratively recaptured and we have to figure them out, lost as they are in the mist of a past which, by definition, cannot be recovered. It is the quantity of pages devoted to the effort of recollecting these hours, without actually reconstructing their actual sequence, it is the disproportion between the time of recollection and the time actually recollected, that produces such a feeling of tender agony and sweet defeat.

Precisely because of this defeat, the final events occur rapidly, in just two chapters. We skip months, and suddenly come to the end. The narrator justifies his quickness by commenting, "What can I say now which is not the story of so many others?" There are only two brief flashbacks. One is by the narrator, telling the actress about his youthful vision of Adrienne (and he is now no longer dreaming, but telling Aurélie a story the reader is already aware of); the other comes from Sylvie, like a thunderbolt, establishing the date of Adrienne's death, as the only real, undeniable fact of the whole story. In the last two chapters the narrator quickens the plot, because there is nothing left of the story to discover. He has given up. This change in pace makes us shift from a time of enchantment to a time of delusion, from a motionless time of dreams to an accelerated time of facts.

Proust was right when he said that this rainbow-hued picture is evoked by music and that it lies not *in* the words but *among* the words. As a matter of fact, it is created by the relationship between plot and story, which commands even the lexical choices of the discourse. If you place the transparent story/plot grid over the discursive surface of the text, you discover that it is exactly in these nodes, when the plot jumps backward in time or returns to the main stream of the narration, that all the changes in tense occur. All these shifts from imperfect to present or past perfect, or from the past perfect continuous to the present and vice versa, are certainly unexpected and frequently imperceptible, but never unmotivated.

Yet as I said in my previous lecture, although I have treated *Sylvie* with almost clinical rigor for years and years, the book has never lost its charm for me. Every time I reread it, it is as if my love affair with Sylvie (I'm not sure whether I mean the book or the character) were beginning for the first time. How can this be possible, since I know the grid, the secret of its strategy? Because the grid can be designed from outside the text, but when you read again, you return inside the text, and—once within it—you cannot read it in haste. Of course you can skim rapidly through the book if, say, you want to retrieve a certain sentence; but in that case you are not reading—you are consulting, scanning, as a computer would. If you are reading, trying to understand the various sentences, you will realize that *Sylvie* forces you to slow down. But as you slow down, as you accept its pace, then you forget any grid or Ariadne's thread, and you get lost again in the woods of Loisy.

Being ill, Labrunie probably did not realize he had constructed such a wonderful narrative mechanism. But the laws of this mechanism lie within the text, before our eyes. How did the fourteenth-century monk Berthold Schwarz, in seeking the philosopher's stone, ever discover gunpowder? He knew nothing about it and did not even want it; but gunpowder exists, unfortunately works, and works according to a chemical formula of which poor Berthold was ignorant. A model reader finds and attributes to the model author what the empirical author might have discovered by pure serendipity.

When I say that Nerval wanted us to understand which structures are used in a text to instruct a model reader, I am making an interpretive conjecture. There are, however, other cases in which the empirical author has directly intervened in order to tell us that he wanted to become exactly that sort of model author. I am thinking of Edgar Allan Poe and his essay "The Philosophy of Composition." Many people took this text as a form of provocation, an attempt to show that in "The Raven" "no one point in its composition is referable either to accident or intuition—that the work proceeded step by step to its completion with the precision and rigid consequence of a mathematical problem." I think that Poe simply wanted to describe what he hoped the first-level reader would feel and the second-level reader would discover in his poem.

We are tempted to consider Poe somewhat naive when he says that a literary work should be short enough to read at one sitting, "for if two sittings be required, the affairs of the world interfere, and everything like totality is at once destroyed." But it seems to me that not even this prescription is based on the psychology of empirical readers: it concerns a model reader's chance to collaborate, and hides the problem of the eternal search for a golden rule. As a second step, Poe reflects on what he considers the main effect of a poem, namely beauty: "Beauty of whatever kind, in its supreme development, invariably excites the sensitive soul to tears. Melancholy is thus the most legitimate of all the poetical tones." But Poe wants to find "some pivot upon which the whole structure might turn" and declares that "no one had been so universally employed as that of the refrain."

Poe dwells at length on the power of the refrain, which derives from the "force of monotone—both in sound and thought," and on the pleasure that "is deduced solely from the sense of identity—of repetition." In the end he decides that, to be monotonously obsessive, the refrain must be "a single word . . . sonorous and susceptible of protracted emphasis," and it seems obvious to him to choose the word "nevermore." But since such a monotonous refrain could not reasonably be attributed to a human being, he feels he has no choice but to put it in the mouth of a speaking animal, the Raven. Then there is another problem to be solved.

> I asked myself—"Of all melancholy topics, what, according to the *universal* understanding of mankind, is the *most* melancholy?" "Death"—was the obvious reply. "And when," I said, "is this most melancholy of topics most poetical?" From what I have already explained at some length, the answer, here also, is obvious—"When it most closely allies itself to *Beauty*." The death, then, of a beautiful woman is, unquestionably, the most poetical topic in the world—and equally is it beyond doubt that the lips best suited to such a topic are those of a bereaved lover.
>
> I had now to combine the two ideas, of a lover lamenting his deceased mistress, and a Raven continuously repeating the word "Nevermore."

Poe forgets nothing, not even the type of rhythm and meter he considers ideal ("the former is trochaic—the latter is octameter acatalectic, alternating with heptameter catalectic repeated in the refrain of the fifth verse, and terminating with tetrameter catalectic"). Finally, he wonders what would be the most opportune way "of bringing together the lover and the Raven." Although it would have been appropriate to have them meet in a forest, a "close circumscription of space" seems to Poe necessary, like "a frame to a picture," to concentrate the attention of the reader. Thus, he places the lover in a room in the lover's own house, and has only to decide how to introduce the bird. "And the thought of introducing him through the window was inevitable." The lover supposes that the flapping of the wings of the bird against the shutter is a tapping at the door, but this detail is designed to prolong the reader's curiosity and "to admit the incidental effect arising from the lover's throwing open the door, finding all dark, and thence adopting the half-fancy that it was the spirit of his mistress that knocked." The night had to be tempestuous (as Snoopy likewise knows very well) "to account for the Raven's seeking admission, and secondly, for the effects of contrast with the (physical) serenity within the chamber." Finally the author decides to have the bird alight on the bust of Pallas, because of the visual contrast between the whiteness of the marble and the blackness of the plumage, "the bust of Pallas being chosen, first, as most in keeping with the scholarship of the lover, and, secondly, for the sonorousness of the word, Pallas, itself."

Need I continue to quote this extraordinary text? Poe is not telling us—as it seems at first—what effects he wants to create in the soul of his empirical readers; otherwise he would have kept quiet about his secret and would have considered the formula of the poem to be as hush-hush as that of Coca-Cola. At most he reveals to us how he produced the effect which is supposed to astound and attract his first-level reader. But in reality he confides to us what he would like his second-level reader to discover.

Should the model reader search for the mythical figure-in-the-carpet celebrated by Henry James? Although one might believe that such a figure is the final meaning of a work of art, it is not the aim here. Poe does not identify the final and univocal meaning of his poem: he describes the strategy he designed to enable a reader to explore his poem endlessly.

Perhaps he decided to reveal his methods because up to that moment he had never come across his ideal reader, and he wanted to act as the best reader of his own poem. If so, his was a pathetic act of tender arrogance and humble pride; he should never have written "The Philosophy of Composition" and should have left *us* the task of understanding his secret. But we know that, so far as his mental health was concerned, Edgar was no better off than Gérard. The latter gave the impression of not knowing anything about what he had done, whereas the former gives the impression of knowing too much. Reticence (Labrunie's mad innocence) and verbosity (Poe's excess of formulas) belong to the psychology of the two empirical authors. But Poe's loquacity permits us to understand Labrunie's reserve. We have to transform the latter into a model author and make him say what he had hidden from us; with the former we have to recognize that, even if the empirical author had not spoken, the model author's strategy would have been very clear from the text. The disquieting figure "on the pallid bust of Pallas" has now become our own discovery. We can wander around that room for ages, as in the forest between Loisy and Châalis, searching for the lost Adrienne-Lenore, wanting never to emerge from those woods again. Nevermore.

LINGERING IN THE WOODS

A certain Monsieur Humblot, in rejecting the manuscript of Proust's *A la Recherche du temps perdu* for the publisher Ollendorff, wrote, "I may be slow on the uptake, but I just can't believe that someone can take thirty pages to describe how you toss and turn in bed before falling asleep."

Calvino, when he praised quickness, cautioned, "I do not wish to say that quickness is a value in itself. Narrative time can also be delaying, cyclic, or motionless . . . This apologia for quickness does not presume to deny the pleasures of lingering."[1] Unless such pleasures existed, we could not admit Proust into the Pantheon of letters.

If, as we have noted, a text is a lazy machine that appeals to the reader to do some of its work, why might a text linger, slow down, take its time? A fictional work, you would suppose, describes people performing actions, and the reader wants to know how these actions turn out. They tell me that in Hollywood, when a producer is listening to the story or plot of a film that is being proposed and finds that there is too much detail, he calls out "Cut to the chase!" And this means: don't waste time, drop the psychological subtleties, get to the climax, when Indiana Jones has a crowd of enemies after him, or when John Wayne and his companions in *Stagecoach* are about to be overwhelmed by Geronimo.

On the other hand we do find, in the old manuals of sexual casuistry which so delighted Huysmans' Des Esseintes, the notion of *delectatio morosa,* a lingering conceded even to those who urgently feel the need to procreate. If something important or gripping is going to take place, we have to cultivate the art of lingering.

In a wood, you go for a walk. If you're not forced to leave it in a hurry to get away from the wolf or the ogre, it is lovely to linger, to watch the beams of sunlight play among the trees and fleck the glades, to examine the moss, the mushrooms, the plants in the undergrowth. Lingering doesn't mean wasting time: frequently one stops to ponder before making a decision.

But since one can wander in a wood without going anywhere in particular, and since at times it's fun to get lost just for the hell of it, I shall be dealing with those walks that the author's strategy induces the reader to take.

One of the lingering or slowing-down techniques that an author can employ is the one that allows the reader to take "inferential walks." I've spoken about this concept in *The Role of the Reader.*[2]

In any work of fiction the text emits signals of suspense, almost as if the discourse slowed down or even came to a halt, and as if the writer were suggesting, "Now *you* try carrying on . . ." When I spoke of "inferential walks" I meant, in the terms of our woodsy metaphor, imaginary walks outside the wood: readers, in order to predict how a story is going to go, turn to their own experience of life or their knowledge of other stories. In the 1950s, *Mad* magazine ran some short comic stories called "Scenes We'd Like to See," of which you have an example in Figure 10.[3] These stories were naturally aimed at frustrating the inferential walks of the reader, who inevitably imagined endings typical of Hollywood films.

But texts are not always so wicked, and are usually inclined to allow the reader the pleasure of making a guess which will then be proved correct. We mustn't, however, make the mistake of

Figure 10

thinking that signals of suspense are typical only of dime novels or of commercial films. The readerly process of making predictions constitutes a necessary emotional aspect of reading which brings into play hopes and fears, as well as the tension that derives from our identification with the fate of the characters.[4]

The masterpiece of nineteenth-century Italian literature is *I promessi sposi* (known in English as *The Betrothed*), by Alessandro Manzoni. Almost all Italians hate it because they were forced to read it in school. My father, however, encouraged me to read *I promessi sposi* before my teachers forced me to, and I love it.

At one point in the book Don Abbondio, a seventeenth-century country curate whose main gift is cowardice, is returning home reciting his breviary and sees "something he did not expect or want to see at all"—that is, two "bravoes" waiting for him. "Bravoes" in those days were mercenaries or adventurers, scoundrels in the service of the Spanish aristocrats who dominated Lombardy, and were employed by their lords in perpetrating the dirtiest of dirty tricks. Another writer might wish to placate our impatience as readers and tell us straight away what happens—might cut to the chase. Not so Manzoni. He does something that the reader may find quite incredible. He takes a few pages, rich in historical detail, to explain who the bravoes were. Having done this, he goes back to Don Abbondio, but he doesn't have him meet the bravoes at once. He keeps us waiting:

> It was only too obvious that the two bravoes we mentioned earlier were waiting for someone; but the thing that Don Abbondio liked least of all was being forced to realize by certain unmistakable signs that they were waiting for him. For as he appeared they looked at each other, raising their heads as they did so in a movement which clearly went with the words "Here he is!" Then the man astride the wall swung his leg over on the track and got up, the other man parted company with the wall against which he had been leaning, and both of them began to walk towards the priest.

Don Abbondio still kept his breviary open in front of him, as if he were reading, but kept peeping over the top of it to see what they were doing. When he saw them coming straight towards him, a dozen unpleasant thoughts struck him at once. First he wondered whether there was a side-turning anywhere between himself and the bravoes, either to the right or the left; but he remembered clearly that no such paths existed. He rapidly searched his mind to see if he had fallen into the sin of offending men of power, or men of vengeance; but even at this moment of distress he could draw a little comfort from the witness of a perfectly clear conscience. And yet the bravoes drew nearer, looking straight at him as they did so. He put the first two fingers of his left hand under his collar, as if to adjust it; and he ran them round his neck, as he turned his head and looked behind him out of the corner of his eye, as far into the distance as he could, twisting his lips at the same time, to see if anyone was coming along from that direction. But there was no one there. He looked over the side wall into the fields, and there was no one there either. He directed a more cautious glance straight ahead, but there was nobody there except the bravoes. What was he to do?[5]

What is to be done? Notice that this question is directly addressed not only to Don Abbondio but also to the reader. Manzoni is a master at mixing his narration with sudden, sly appeals to the reader, and this is one of the less sneaky. What would you have done in Don Abbondio's place? This is a typical example of how a model author, or the text, can invite the reader to take an inferential walk. The delaying tactics serve to stimulate this walk. Note, further, that readers are not supposed to ask themselves what is to be done, because it's obvious that Don Abbondio has no means of escape. Readers may likewise put two fingers under their collar—not to adjust it but to glance forward in the story. They are invited to wonder what two bravoes want with a man so innocuous and normal. Well, I'm not going to tell you. If you haven't read *The Betrothed*, it's time you did. You should know, however, that everything in the novel stems from this meeting.

Still, we might ask ourselves if it was necessary for Manzoni to insert those pages of historical information on the bravoes. The reader is tempted to skip them, of course, and every reader of *The Betrothed* has done so, at least the first time. And yet, even the time needed to turn the pages we don't read is taken into account by the narrative strategy, because the model author knows (even if the empirical author wouldn't know how to express it conceptually) that in a work of fiction time appears in three forms—namely, story time, discourse time, and reading time.

Story time is part of the content of the story. If the text says "a thousand years pass," the story time is a thousand years. But at the level of linguistic expression, which is at the level of fictional discourse, the time to write (and read) the utterance is very short. This is why a rapid *discourse time* may express a very long story time. Of course the opposite may also occur: we saw in the preceding lecture that Nerval needed twelve chapters to tell us what happened in a night and a day, and then in two short chapters he told us what happened in the course of months and years.

Theorists of fiction all more or less agree that it is easy to establish the story time.[6] Jules Verne's *Around the World in Eighty Days*, from the time of departure to the time of arrival, lasts eighty days—at least for the members of the Reform Club, waiting in London (for Phileas Fogg, who is traveling eastward, it lasts eighty-one). But it is less easy to determine the discourse time. Should we base it on the length of the written text, or on the time needed to read it? We cannot be sure that these two durations are exactly in proportion. If we had to work it out from the number of words, the two passages I'm now going to read you would both be examples of the narrative phenomenon Gérard Genette calls "isochrony" and Seymour Chatman calls "scene"—that is, where story and discourse are of relatively equal duration, as happens with dialogues. The first example comes from a typical hard-boiled novel, a narrative genre where everything is reduced to action and the reader is not allowed a moment's respite. The ideal description in the hard-boiled novel is that of the St. Valentine's Day massacre: a few seconds, and all the enemies are liquidated. Mickey Spillane, who in this sense was the Al Capone of literature, at the end of *One Lonely Night* describes a scene which had to happen in a few instants:

> They heard my scream and the awful roar of the gun and the slugs tearing into bone and guts and it was the last they heard. They went down as they tried to run and felt their insides tear out and spray against the wall. I saw the general's head splinter into shiny wet fragments and splatter over the floor. The guy from the subway tried to stop the bullets with his hands and dissolved into a nightmare of blue holes.[7]

I might have been able to carry out the massacre just before I finished reading the passage out loud, but we can be reasonably satisfied. Twenty-six seconds of reading for ten seconds of massacre is pretty good going. In films, we usually have a precise match between discourse time and story time—a good example of *scene.*

But now let's see how Ian Fleming describes another horrifying event, the death of Le Chiffre in *Casino Royale.*

> There was a sharp "phut," no louder than a bubble of air escaping from a tube of toothpaste. No other noise at all, and suddenly Le Chiffre had grown another eye, a third eye on a level with the other two, right where the thick nose started to jut out below the forehead. It was a small black eye, without eyelashes or eyebrows. For a second the three eyes looked out across the room and then the whole face seemed to slip and go down on one knee. The two outer eyes turned trembling up towards the ceiling.[8]

The story lasts two seconds, one for Bond to shoot and the other for Le Chiffre to stare at the room with his three eyes, but the reading of this description took me forty-two seconds. Forty-two seconds for ninety-eight words in Fleming is proportionately slower than twenty-six seconds for eighty-one words in Spillane. Reading aloud has helped give you the impression of a sloweddown description, which in a film (for example, in Sam Peckinpah's movies) would likewise have lasted quite a while, as if time had stopped. With the Spillane passage I was tempted to accelerate the rhythm of my reading, whereas reading Fleming I slowed down. I would say that Fleming's is a good example of "stretching," in which the discourse slows down in comparison to the speed of the story. Yet the stretching, like the scene, depends not on the number of words but on the *pace* that the text imposes on the reader. Moreover, in the course of a silent reading one is tempted to go quickly through Spillane, whereas one is led to savor Fleming (if we can use this word for such an appalling description). The terms, the metaphors, the ways the reader's attention is fixed, force the Fleming reader to look in a very unusual way at a man who receives a bullet in his forehead; in contrast, the expressions used by Spillane evoke visions of massacre that already belong to our reader or spectator memories. We must admit that the comparison of the noise of a pistol's silencer to that of a bubble of air, and the metaphor of the third eye, and the two natural eyes that at a certain point look up to where the third cannot, are an example of that *defamiliarization* extolled by the Russian Formalists.

In his essay on Flaubert's style,[9] Proust says that one of the virtues of Flaubert is that he knows how to render the impression of time exceptionally well. And Proust, who took thirty pages to describe someone tossing and turning in his bed, enthusiastically admires the ending of *The Sentimental Education,* of which the finest thing, he maintains, is not a sentence but a white space.

Proust observes that Flaubert, who has spent a great many pages describing the most insignificant actions of his protagonist Frédéric Moreau, accelerates toward the end, where he presents one of the most dramatic moments of Frédéric's life. After Louis-Napoleon's coup d'état, Frédéric witnesses a cavalry charge in the center of Paris, observes excitedly the arrival of a squadron of dragoons "bent over their horses, with their swords drawn," sees a policeman, sword in hand, attack a rebel, who falls down dead. "The policeman looked all around him, and Frédéric, open-mouthed, recognized Sénécal."

At this point Flaubert ends the chapter, and the white space which follows seems to Proust an "enormous blank." Then, "without the shadow of a transition, while the measurement of time suddenly becomes no longer a quarter of an hour but years, decades," Flaubert writes:

> He travelled.
> He came to know the melancholy of the steamboat, the cold awakening in the tent, the tedium of landscape and ruins, the bitterness of interrupted friendship.
> He returned.
> He went into society, and he had other lovers. But the ever-present memory of the first made them insipid: and besides, the violence of desire, the very flower of feeling, had gone.[10]

We could say that Flaubert has step-by-step accelerated the discourse time, initially in order to render the acceleration of events (or of the story time). But then, after the blank space, he inverts the procedure and produces a very long story time in a very short discourse time. I think that here we see an example of defamiliarization which is obtained not semantically but syntactically and in which the reader is forced to "shift gears" through that simple but enormous blank space.

So the discourse time is the result of a textual strategy that interacts with the response of readers and forces a reading time on them.

At this point we can return to the question we asked about Manzoni. Why did he insert those pages of historical information on the bravoes, knowing full well that the reader would skip them? Because even the act of skipping takes time, or at least gives the impression of taking some time in order to save more. Readers know they are skipping (though perhaps they silently promise to read those pages afterward) and must infer or be aware that they are skipping pages which contain essential information. The author is not just suggesting to the reader that facts like the ones he is narrating actually happened; he is also indicating to what extent that little story is rooted in History. If one understands this (even if one has skipped the pages on the bravoes), Don Abbondio's gesture of fingering his collar becomes a great deal more dramatic.

How can a text impose a reading pace on a reader? We shall understand this better if we think about what happens in architecture and in the figurative arts.

Usually it is said that there exist forms of art where the duration of time plays a specific role and where the discourse time coincides with the "reading time"; this happens in music, above all, and in film. In film the discourse time does not necessarily coincide with the story time, whereas in music there is perfect congruence among the three times (except if one wants to identify the story with the theme or the melodic sequence, and both plot and discourse with a complex treatment of these themes, through variations or flashbacks to early themes, as in Wagner). These temporal arts permit only a "rereading time," since the viewer or the listener can listen or watch over and over again—and today records, tapes, compact discs, and videocassettes have enormously expanded this privilege.

In contrast, it seems that the arts of space, such as painting and architecture, have nothing to do with time. Certainly they can embody formal evidence of their physical aging over the centuries (they tell us about their history), but they do not seem to allow time for being enjoyed. Even a visual work of art, however, requires a *circumnavigational time*. Both sculpture and architecture require—and impose through the complexity of their structure—a minimum time to be entirely experienced. One could take a year to circumnavigate the cathedral at Chartres, without ever realizing how many sculptural and architectural details there are to be discovered. The Beinecke Library at

Yale, with its four identical sides and its symmetrical windows, requires less time to circumnavigate than does Chartres cathedral. Rich architectural decoration represents an imposition of the architectural form on viewers, since the richer the detail, the more time it takes to enjoy it. Certain pictorial works of art require multiple viewings. Take, for example, a painting by Jackson Pollock: here the canvas is, at first glance, open to a quick inspection (the viewer sees only informal matter), but upon subsequent inspection the work must be interpreted as the fixed trace of the process of its own formation, and—as happens in a wood or in a labyrinth—it is difficult to tell which path is the privileged one, where to start, which way to choose so as to penetrate the still image that results from the act of dripping the paint.

In written fiction it is certainly difficult to ascertain what the discourse time and the reading time may be; but there is no doubt that at times an abundance of description, a mass of minute particulars in the narration, may serve less as a representational device than as a strategy for slowing down the reading time, until the reader drops into the rhythm that the author believes necessary to the enjoyment of the text.

There are certain works that, in order to impose this rhythm on the reader, make story time, discourse time, and reading time identical. In television this would be referred to as *live broadcast*. Just think of that film in which Andy Warhol trained a camera on the Empire State Building for a whole day. It is difficult in literature to quantify reading time, but it could be argued that in reading the last chapter of *Ulysses* you need at least as much time as Molly took to think through her stream of consciousness. At other times all we need to do is use proportional criteria: if you take two pages of text to say that someone has gone a mile, you'll need four pages to say that he has gone two miles.

That great literary trickster Georges Perec once nurtured the ambition of writing a book as big as the world. Then he realized he couldn't manage it, and in *Tentative d'épuisement d'un lieu parisien* he more humbly tried to describe "live" everything that had happened in the place Saint-Sulpice from October 18 to October 20, 1974. Perec knew perfectly well that many things have been written about that square, but he set out to describe the rest, what no history book or novel has ever told: the totality of everyday life. He sits down on a bench, or in one of the two bars of the square, and for two whole days writes down everything that he sees—the buses that go by, a Japanese tourist who photographs him, a man in a green raincoat; he notices that the passersby have at least one hand occupied, holding a bag, a briefcase, the hand of a child, a dog's leash; he even records seeing someone who looks like the actor Peter Sellers. At two P.M. on October 20, he stops. It is quite impossible to tell everything that happens at a certain spot in the world, and when all is said and done, his own account is sixty pages long and can be read in half an hour. That is, if the reader doesn't savor it slowly for a couple of days, trying to imagine every scene described. At this point, however, we would be talking not about reading time but about hallucinating time. In the same way we can use a map to imagine trips and extraordinary adventures through unknown lands and seas, but in such a case the map has become merely a stimulus and the reader has become the narrator. Whenever I'm asked what book I would take with me to a desert island, I reply, "The phone book: with all those characters, I could invent an infinite number of stories."

Congruence among story, discourse, and reading times may be sought for reasons which have very little to do with art. Lingering is not always an index of nobility. I once asked myself how one could scientifically ascertain whether a film was pornographic or not. A moralist would reply that a film is pornographic if it contains explicit and detailed scenes of sexual acts. But in many pornography trials it has been demonstrated that certain works of art contain such scenes for realistic purposes, to describe life as it is, or for ethical reasons (insofar as the sensuality shown is condemned), and that in any case the aesthetic value of the entire work redeems the obscenity of its parts. Since it's hard to establish whether an author is truly concerned with realism, or has sincere ethical intentions, or attains aesthetically satisfying results, I decided (after examining many hard-core movies) that an infallible rule does exist.

When trying to assess a film that contains sexually explicit scenes, you should check to see whether, when a character gets into an elevator or a car, the discourse time coincides with the story time. Flaubert may take one line to say that Frédéric traveled for a long time, and in normal films a character who gets on a plane at Logan Airport in Boston will, in the next scene, land in San Francisco. But in a pornographic film if someone gets in a car to go ten blocks, the car will journey those ten blocks in real time. If someone opens a fridge and pours out a Sprite that he's going to drink in the armchair after switching on the TV, the action takes precisely the time it would take you if you were doing the same thing at home.

The reason is pretty simple. A pornographic film is designed to satisfy the audience's desire for sexually explicit scenes, but it can't show an hour and a half of uninterrupted sexual acts because that would be tiring for the actors—and ultimately tedious for the audience as well. The sexual acts therefore have to be dispersed throughout the story. But no one has the least intention of spending time and money thinking up a worthwhile story, and the spectators aren't interested in the story either, because all they're doing is waiting for the sexy bits. The story is thereby reduced to a series of insignificant everyday actions, such as going someplace, drinking a whisky, putting on a coat, talking about irrelevant things; and it makes more economic sense to film someone driving a car than to mix him up in a shoot-out à la Mickey Spillane (which, apart from everything else, would distract the viewer). And so, whatever is not sexually explicit has to take as much time as it would in everyday life—whereas the sexual acts have to take *longer* than they would in reality. This, then, is the rule: when in a film two characters take the same time they would in real life to get from A to B, we can be absolutely sure we are dealing with a pornographic film. Of course, sexually explicit acts are also required—otherwise a film like Wim Wenders' *Im Lauf der Zeit,* or *Kings of the Road* (1976), where two people are shown traveling on a truck for the better part of four hours, would be a pornographic film, which is not the case.

Dialogue is often cited as the prime example of perfect congruence between story time and discourse time. But the following is a rather exceptional case, in which, for reasons that have nothing to do with literature, an author has managed to invent a dialogue that gives the impression of lasting longer than a real one. Alexandre Dumas used to be paid by the line for his novels, which were published in installments, and so he was often led to increase the number of lines to add a little something to his income. In Chapter 11 of *The Three Musketeers* (to which we shall return in another lecture) d'Artagnan meets his beloved Constance Bonacieux, suspects her of unfaithfulness, and tries to discover why she was found at night near Aramis' house. Here is a part, and only a part, of the dialogue that comes at this point in the novel:

> "Without doubt, Aramis is one of my most intimate friends."
> "Aramis! Who is he?"
> "Come, come, you won't tell me you don't know Aramis?"
> "This is the first time I ever heard his name pronounced."
> "It is the first time, then, that you ever went to that house?"
> "Certainly it is."
> "And you did not know that it was inhabited by a young man?"
> "No."
> "By a musketeer?"
> "Not at all."
> "It was not him, then, you came to seek?"
> "Not the least in the world. Besides, you must have seen that the person I spoke to was a woman."

"That is true; but this woman may be one of the friends of Aramis."

"I know nothing of that."

"Since she lodges with him."

"That does not concern me."

"But who is she?"

"Oh! That is not my secret."

"My dear Madame Bonacieux, you are charming; but at the same time you are one of the most mysterious women."

"Do I lose much by that?"

"No; you are, on the contrary, adorable!"

"Give me your arm, then."

"Most willingly. And now?"

"Now conduct me."

"Where?"

"Where I am going."

"But where are you going?"

"You will see, because you will leave me at the door."

"Shall I wait for you?"

"That will be useless."

"You will return alone, then?"

"Perhaps I may, perhaps I may not."

"But will the person who shall accompany you afterward be a man or a woman?"

"I don't know yet."

"But I will know it!"

"How?"

"I will wait for your coming out."

"In that case, adieu!"

"Why so?"

"I do not want you."

"But you have claimed . . ."

"The aid of a gentleman, not the watchfulness of a spy."

"The word is rather hard."

"How are they called who follow others in spite of them?"

"They are indiscreet."

"The word is too mild."

"Well, madame, I perceive I must act as you please."

"Why did you deprive yourself of the merit of doing so at once?"

"Is there no merit in repentance?"

"And you do really repent?"

"I know nothing about myself. But what I know is, that I promise to do all you wish if you will allow me to accompany you where you are going."

"And you will leave me afterward?"

"Yes."

"Without waiting for my coming out again?"

"No."

"Parole d'honneur?"

"By the faith of a gentleman."

"Take my arm, then, and let us go on."[11]

Certainly we know other instances of lengthy and irrelevant dialogue—for example, in Ionesco or in Ivy Compton-Burnett—but in those cases the dialogue is inconsistent because it is designed to represent irrelevance. In Dumas' case a jealous lover and a lady who must run to meet Lord Buckingham to bring him to the Queen of France should not waste time in such *marivaudages*. This is not "functional" lingering; it is more similar to the deceleration found in pornographic films.

And yet Dumas was a master at constructing narrative lingering which aims to create what I would call *trepidation time*—that is, it delays the arrival of a dramatic ending. And in this sense *The Count of Monte Cristo* is a masterpiece. Aristotle had already stipulated that catastrophe and catharsis should be preceded by long peripeties.

In John Sturges' excellent film *Bad Day at Black Rock* (1954), a veteran of the Second World War, a mild-mannered fellow with a crippled left arm, played by Spencer Tracy, comes to a town in the middle of nowhere to find the father of a dead Japanese soldier, and becomes the object of unbearable daily persecution by racist bad guys. Viewers of the film identify with Tracy's agony and yearn for an impossible revenge, undergoing an hour of intolerable frustration . . . At a certain point, while he's having a drink in a luncheonette, Tracy is provoked by a hateful individual, and suddenly that forbearing man makes a rapid movement with his good arm and strikes the enemy a powerful blow: the bad guy is hurled the whole length of the place and flung out into the street after smashing through the door. This act of violence comes quite unexpectedly, but it's been prepared for by such a slow series of extremely painful outrages that it acquires cathartic value for the spectators, who finally relax in their seats. If they had to wait less time and if their trepidation were less intense, the catharsis wouldn't be so complete.

Italy is one of those countries in which one is allowed to enter a cinema at any time during the show and then stay to see it again from the beginning. I think this is a good custom, because I hold that a film is much like life in a certain respect: I entered into this life with my parents already born and Homer's *Odyssey* already written, and then I tried to work out the story going backward, as I did with *Sylvie,* until I more or less understood what had happened in the world before I arrived. So it seems quite right to me to do the same thing with films. The night I saw *Bad Day at Black Rock,* I noticed that after Spencer Tracy's violent gesture (which doesn't occur at the end of the film) half of the audience got up and left. They were spectators who had come in at the start of that *delectatio morosa* and had stayed on to enjoy the preparatory phases of that moment of liberation all over again. From this you can see that the trepidation time functions not only to keep the attention of the naive first-level spectator, but also to stimulate the aesthetic enjoyment of the second-level spectator.

In point of fact, I wouldn't want you to think that these techniques (which are of course more clearly evident in works that are none too complex) belong just to popular art or literature. Indeed, I would like to show you an example of lingering on an epic scale, spread over hundreds of pages, whose function is to prepare us for a moment of satisfaction and joy without end, compared to which the pleasures of a pornographic film pale into insignificance. I'm referring to Dante Alighieri's *Divine Comedy*. And if we speak about Dante here, we have to think about and even try to become his model reader—a medieval reader, who firmly believed that one's earthly pilgrimage should culminate in that moment of supreme ecstasy which is the vision of God.

But this reader approached Dante's poem as if it were fictional, and Dorothy Sayers was right when she recommended, in introducing her translation of the work, that the ideal way of reading it would be "to start at the first line and go straight through to the end, surrendering to the vigour of the story-telling and the swift movement of the verse." Readers must be aware that they are following a slow exploration of all the circles of Hell, through the center of the Earth, then up to the terraces and cornices of Mount Purgatory, and then higher still, beyond the earthly paradise, "from sphere to sphere of the singing Heavens, beyond the planets, beyond the stars, beyond the Primum Mobile, into the Empyrean, there to behold God as He is."[12]

This voyage is none other than an interminable lingering, in the course of which we meet hundreds of characters; are involved in conversations about contemporary politics, about theology, about life and death; and witness scenes of suffering, melancholy, and joy. We often find ourselves wanting to skip passages in order to speed things up, but in skipping we know all the time that the poet is slowing down, and we almost turn around to wait for him to catch up with us. And all this for what? To get to that moment when Dante will see something he is unable to express adequately—that point "Where speech is vanquished and must lag behind—And memory surrenders in such plight."

In that abyss I saw how love held bound
Into one volume all the lives whose flight
Is scattered through the universe around;
How substance, accident, and mode unite,
Fused, so to speak, together in such wise
That this I tell is one simple light.[13]

Dante says that he's unable to express what he has seen (even though he's managed it better than anyone else) and indirectly asks his readers to use their imagination, there where his "high phantasy lost power." His readers are satisfied: they have been waiting for that moment when they would find themselves face to face with the Unutterable. And to experience that emotion, with its interminable lingering, the long preceding voyage is necessary. But these are delays during which time is not wasted: while we wait for an encounter which can only dissolve into a dazzling silence, we learn a great deal about the world—which is, after all, the best thing that can happen to us in this life.

Often, fictional delays comprise descriptions of objects, characters, or landscapes. The problem is determining what use these are to the story. In an old essay of mine on the James Bond novels,[14] I pointed out that Ian Fleming reserves his long descriptions for a game of golf, for a car race, for a girl's meditations on the sailor who appears on a packet of Player's cigarettes, for the crawling of an insect; whereas more dramatic events like an assault on Fort Knox or a life-and-death struggle with a killer shark are related in a few pages or even at times a few lines. I deduced from this that the only function of these descriptions is to persuade readers that they are reading a work of art, because people generally believe that the difference between low-brow and high-brow literature lies in the fact that the latter is full of long descriptions, whereas the former cuts to the chase. Furthermore, Fleming lavishes description primarily on actions that readers could engage in themselves (a card game, a dinner, a

Turkish bath) and compresses his accounts of those actions that readers would never dream of being able to do, such as escaping from a castle by hanging onto an aeronautic balloon. Lingering over the *déjà vu* allows the reader to identify with Bond and to dream of being like him.

Fleming slows down on the superfluous and quickens the pace when it comes to the essential because slowing down on the superfluous is the erotic function of the *delectatio morosa,* and because he knows that we know that stories told excitedly are the most dramatic. Manzoni, like the good nineteenth-century romantic novelist that he is, uses basically the same strategy as Fleming, although well before him, and he makes us wait agonizingly for each event to occur; but he doesn't waste time on the inessential. The Don Abbondio who puts his fingers nervously under his collar and asks himself what is to be done is an emblem of seventeenth-century Italian society under foreign domination. The thoughts of an adventuress pondering a packet of cigarettes don't tell us very much about the culture of our time (we learn only that she is a dreamer or a snob), whereas Manzoni's lingering over the uncertainty of Don Abbondio explains a lot of things about Italy—not only in the seventeenth century but in the twentieth, too.

Elsewhere, though, the descriptive lingering may have another function. There's also something that I call *hint time.* Saint Augustine, who was a subtle reader of texts, wondered why the Bible tended to devote so many words to *superfluous* descriptions of clothes, buildings, perfumes, and jewelry. Was it possible that God, the inspirer of the biblical writer, could waste so much time indulging in mundane poetry? Obviously not. If there were indeed sudden slowing-down moments in the text, it was because the Holy Scripture was trying to make us realize that we should interpret those descriptions allegorically or symbolically.

I do beg your pardon, but I must return to Nerval's *Sylvie.* You will remember that the writer, in Chapter 2, after sleepless hours spent evoking the years of his youth, decides to leave for Loisy during the night. But he doesn't know what time it is. Is it possible that a rich young man, cultured, a lover of the theater, doesn't have a clock in his house? Believe it or not, he doesn't have one. Or rather, he does have one, but it doesn't work. And yet Nerval spends a page describing it:

> Among the bric-à-brac splendors which it was then customary to collect, in order to give local color to an old-fashioned apartment, there shone the restored brilliance of one of those tortoiseshell Renaissance pendulum-clocks, whose gilded dome surmounted by the figure of Time is supported by caryatids in the Medici style, resting in their turn on half-rearing horses. The historical Diana, leaning on her stag, appears in low relief under the face, where the enameled figures of the hours are displayed on an inlaid background. The works, excellent no doubt, had not been wound up for two centuries. It was not to tell the time that I had bought that clock in Touraine.

Here is a case where the lingering is designed not so much to slow down the action, to push the reader into taking exciting inferential walks, as it is to indicate that we must prepare ourselves to enter a world in which the normal measurement of time counts for next to nothing, a world in which clocks have broken down or been liquefied, as in a Dali painting.

But in *Sylvie* we also have time for getting lost. This is why I said in my previous lectures that whenever I go back to *Sylvie* I forget everything I knew about the text and lose myself again in the labyrinth of time. Nerval can apparently wander off for five pages evoking Rousseau on the ruins of Ermenonville, and certainly all of his digressions help us toward a fuller understanding of the story, of the era, of the character. But above all, this digressing and lingering helps to enclose readers within those time-woods from which they can escape only after the most strenuous efforts (and which they will then want to get back into again).

I promised that I would talk about Chapter 7 of *Sylvie*. The narrator, after a couple of flashbacks, to which we managed to assign a place in the story, is arriving at Loisy. It's four in the morning. The scene is apparently the evening in 1838 when he is returning to Loisy, now a grown-up, and he describes the landscape through which the carriage passes, using the present tense. Suddenly he remembers, "It was along there that Sylvie's brother drove me one evening . . ." What evening? Before or after the second party at Loisy? We'll never know, and we mustn't know. The narrator switches back to the present tense and describes the place as it looks that evening, but as it might still be at the moment he's telling the story, and it's a place that richly evokes the Medici, like the clock a few pages earlier. Then he returns to the imperfect tense, and Adrienne appears—for the second and last time in the story. She looks like an actress on a stage, in a holy play, "transfigured by her costume as she already was by her vocation" (she has become a nun). The vision is so vague that at this point the narrator expresses doubts which permeate the entire story: "As I retrace these details, I begin to wonder whether they were real or whether I dreamed them." And then he asks himself if the apparition of Adrienne was as real as the incontestable existence of the Abbey of Châalis. Returning suddenly to the present tense, he muses, "Perhaps this memory is an obsession . . ." Now the carriage is approaching the real Loisy, and the narrator escapes from the realm of reverie.

Well! A long narrative lingering to say nothing—or nothing concerning the development of the story. To say only that time, memory, and dream can melt together and that the reader's duty is to be captured by the whirl of their unresolved struggle.

But there is also a way of lingering in the text, and of "wasting" time, so as to render the idea of space. One of the least precise and least analyzed of rhetorical figures is *hypotyposis*. How can a verbal text put something before our eyes as if we could see it? I would like to conclude this lecture by suggesting that one way of rendering the impression of space is to expand both the discourse time and the reading time in relation to the story time.

One of the questions that has always intrigued Italian readers is why Manzoni spends so much time, at the start of *The Betrothed*, in describing Lake Como. We can forgive Proust for taking thirty pages to describe the process of getting to sleep, but why does Manzoni have to take at least a page to tell us, "Once upon a time there was a lake and here I intend to set my story"? If we tried reading this passage with a map before us, we would see that Manzoni builds his description by combining two film techniques: zoom and slow motion. Don't tell me that a nineteenth-century writer didn't know about film techniques: on the contrary, movie directors make use of the techniques of literary fiction. Manzoni proceeds as if he were filming from a helicopter slowly landing (or as if he were reproducing the way God looks down from the heavens to single out a human individual on the earth's surface). This first continuous movement downward from on high begins in a "geographical" dimension:

> One arm of Lake Como turns off to the south between two unbroken chains of mountains, which cut it up into a series of bays and inlets as the hills advance into the water and retreat again, until it quite suddenly grows much narrower and takes on the appearance and the motion of a river between a headland on one side and a wide stretch of shore on the other.

But then the vision abandons the geographical dimension to change slowly to a "topographical" one, at the point where you can begin to distinguish a bridge and the banks:

> The bridge which connects the two banks at that point seems to make the change of state still clearer to the eye, marking the spot where the lake comes to an end and the Adda comes into being once more—though further on it again takes the name of a lake, as the banks separate, allowing the water to spread out and lose its speed among more bays and fresh inlets.

The geographical and topographical visions both proceed from north to south, following the course of the river; and the description thus moves from wide angle to narrow: from the lake to the river and then to the streams, from the mountaintops to the slopes and then to the little valleys. And as this happens, the "film" starts moving in a different way, this time not descending from the geographical to the topographical, but expanding from depth to width: at this point the mountains are seen in profile and the perspective alters, as if a human being were looking at them at last.

> The stretch of shore we mentioned is formed by the silt from three considerable streams, and is backed by two adjoining mountains, one known as St. Martin's Mount, and the other by the Lombard-sounding name of Resegone because of the many small peaks that make up its skyline, which do in fact give it the look of a saw. This is enough of a distinctive sign to make the Resegone easy to pick out from the long and vast chains of other mountains, less well known by name and less strange in shape, in which it lies, even if the observer has never seen it before— provided that he sees it from an angle which shows its full length, as for example looking northward from the walls of Milan.

Now, when the description has attained a human scale, we as readers can discern the smallest detail of every road. I would say more: we experience all the tactile sensations we would feel if we were marching upon those very pebbles.

> The slope up from the water's edge is gentle and unbroken for quite a long way: but then it breaks up into mounds and gullies, terraces and steeper tracts . . . Along the extreme fringe of the slope, the terrain is deeply cut up by watercourses, and consists mostly of gravel and pebbles; but the rest of the area is all fields and vineyards with townships, estates and hamlets here and there. There are also some woods, which extend upwards into

the mountains. Lecco is the largest of the townships, and gives its name to the territory.[15]

Here Manzoni makes another choice: he passes from topography to history, beginning to tell us about the city of Lecco. Then he shifts from collective history to the individual story of Don Abbondio, whom we finally meet "along one of those tracks" as he moves toward that fatal meeting with the bravoes.

Manzoni begins his description by assuming the viewpoint of God, the Great Geographer, and little by little assumes the viewpoint of the human beings who live in the landscape. But the fact that he seems to abandon the divine perspective should not fool us. At the end of the novel, if not before, we come to the realization that we are being told not just the story of some poor little human beings but the History of Divine Providence, which directs, corrects, saves, and resolves. The beginning of *The Betrothed* is not an exercise in literary self-indulgence; it's a way of preparing the reader straightaway to read a book whose main protagonist is someone who looks at the ways of the world from on high.

I said that we could read the opening passages looking first at a geographical map and then at a topographical one. But this isn't necessary. If you read properly, you will realize that Manzoni is designing a map; he is setting up a space. Looking at the world with the eyes of his creator, Manzoni competes with Him: he is constructing his fictional world by borrowing aspects of the real one.

A process that we shall hear more about *(flashforward)* in the next lecture.

FOUR

POSSIBLE WOODS

Once upon a time there was . . . "a King!" my gentle audience will immediately exclaim. That's right; this time you've guessed correctly. Once upon a time there was Vittorio Emanuele III, the last king of Italy, sent into exile after the war. This king did not have much of a reputation for humanistic culture, being more interested in economic and military problems, although he was a keen collector of ancient coins. The story goes that one day he had to open a painting exhibition. Finding himself in front of a beautiful landscape showing a valley with a village running along the slopes of a hill, he looked at the little painted village for a long time, then turned to the director of the exhibition and asked: "How many inhabitants does it have?"

The basic rule in dealing with a work of fiction is that the reader must tacitly accept a fictional agreement, which Coleridge called "the suspension of disbelief." The reader has to know that what is being narrated is an imaginary story, but he must not therefore believe that the writer is telling lies. According to John Searle, the author simply *pretends* to be telling the truth.[1] We accept the fictional agreement and we *pretend* that what is narrated has really taken place.

Having had the experience of writing a couple of novels which have reached a few million readers, I have become familiar with an extraordinary phenomenon. For the first few tens of thousands of copies (the figure may vary from country to country), readers generally know perfectly well about this fictional agreement. Afterward, and certainly beyond the first-million mark, you get into a no-man's-land where one can no longer be sure that readers know about it.

In Chapter 115 of my book *Foucault's Pendulum* the character called Casaubon, on the night of the twenty-third to the twenty-fourth of June 1984, after attending an occultist ceremony at the Conservatoire des Arts et Métiers in Paris, walks, as if possessed, along the entire length of the rue Saint-Martin, crosses the rue aux Ours, passes the Centre Beaubourg, and arrives at Saint-Merry Church. Afterward he continues along various streets, all of them named, until he gets to the place des Vosges. In order to write this chapter I walked the same route on several different nights, carrying a tape recorder, taking notes on what I could see and the impressions I had.

Indeed, since I have a computer program which can show me what the sky looks like at any time in any year, at whatever longitude or latitude, I even went so far as to find out if there had been a moon that night, and what position it occupied in the sky at various times. I did this not because I wanted to emulate Emile Zola's realism, but because I like to have the scene I'm writing about in front of me while I narrate; it makes me more familiar with what's happening and helps me get inside the characters.

After publishing the novel, I received a letter from a man who had evidently gone to the Bibliothèque Nationale to read all the newspapers from June 24, 1984. He had discovered that on the corner of the rue Réaumur (which I hadn't actually named but which does cross the rue Saint-Martin at a certain point), after midnight, more or less at the time Casaubon passed by, there had been a fire—and a big fire at that, if the papers had talked about it. The reader asked me how Casaubon had managed not to see it.

To amuse myself, I answered that Casaubon had probably seen the fire but that he hadn't mentioned it for some mysterious reason, unknown to me—a pretty likely explanation, given that the story was so thick with mysteries both true and false. I think that my reader is still trying to find out why Casaubon kept quiet about the fire, probably suspecting another conspiracy by the Knights Templars.

But that reader—even though affected by a sort of mild paranoia—was not entirely mistaken. I had led him to believe that my story took place in "real" Paris, and had even indicated the day. If in the course of such a minute description I had said that next to the Conservatoire stood Gaudí's Sagrada Familia, the reader would have been right to get annoyed, because if we are in Paris we are not in Barcelona. Did our reader really have the right to go looking for a fire which had actually taken place in Paris that night but which wasn't in my book?

I maintain that my reader was exaggerating when he pretended that a fictional story should wholly match the actual world it refers to; but the problem is not quite as simple as that. Before passing final judgment, let's have a look at just how guilty King Vittorio Emanuele III was.

When we enter the fictional wood we are certainly supposed to sign a fictional agreement with the author, and we are ready to accept, say, that wolves speak; but when Little Red Riding Hood is eaten by the wolf, we think she's dead (and this conviction is vital to the reader's extraordinary pleasure in her resurrection). We think of the wolf as shaggy and pointy-eared, more or less like the wolves one finds in real woods, and it seems quite natural that Little Red Riding Hood behaves like a little girl and her Mummy like a grown-up, worried and responsible. Why? Because that's what happens in the world of our experience, a world that for now, without too many ontological commitments, we'll call the *actual world.*

What I'm saying may seem very obvious, but it isn't if we are hanging on to our dogma of suspension of disbelief. It would appear that when reading a work of fiction we suspend our disbelief about some things but not others. And given that the boundaries between what we have to believe in and what we don't are pretty ambiguous (as we shall see), how can we condemn poor old Vittorio Emanuele? If he was merely supposed to admire the aesthetic elements of the picture (its colors, the quality of the perspective), he was quite wrong to ask how many inhabitants the village had. But if he entered it as one enters a fictional world and imagined himself wandering through those hills, why shouldn't he have asked himself whom he would meet there and whether he might find a quiet little inn? Given that the picture was probably a realistic one, why should he have thought that the village was uninhabited, or plagued by nightmares à la Lovecraft? This is really the attraction in every fiction, whether verbal or visual. Such a work encloses us within the boundaries of its world and leads us, one way or another, to take it seriously.

At the end of the previous lecture we noted the way in which Manzoni, describing the Lake of Como, went about constructing a world. Yet he was borrowing the geographical characteristics of the real world. You may think that this happens only in a historical novel. We have seen, however, that it happens even in a fable—though in a fable the proportions between reality and invention are different.

> As Gregor Samsa awoke one morning from uneasy dreams, he found himself transformed in his bed into a gigantic insect.

A nice beginning to a story which is certainly quite fantastic! Either we believe it or we'll have to throw away the whole of Kafka's "Metamorphosis." But let's carry on with our reading.

> He was lying on his hard, as it were armour-plated, back and when he lifted his head a little he could see his dome-like brown belly divided into stiff arched segments on top of which the bed-quilt could hardly keep in position and was about to slide off completely. His numerous legs, which were pitifully thin compared to the rest of his bulk, waved helplessly before his eyes.

This description seems to intensify the unbelievable nature of what has happened, yet reduces it to acceptable proportions. It's amazing that a man wakes up to find himself transformed into an insect; but if in fact he has done so, this insect must have the normal features of a normal insect. These few lines of Kafka's are an example of realism, not surrealism. We just have to pretend to believe that this ordinary insect is "gigantic," which is actually quite a tall order for the fictional agreement. On the other hand, even Gregor can hardly believe his own eyes: "What has happened to me?" he asks himself. As we ourselves would in a similar situation. But let's go on. The follow-up to the description is by no means fantastic but is absolutely realistic:

> It was no dream. His room, a regular human bedroom, only rather too small, lay quiet between the four familiar walls . . .[2]

And the description continues, presenting a bedroom like many others we have encountered. Further on, it will seem absurd that Gregor's parents and sister, without asking themselves too many questions, accept that their relative has become an insect, but their reaction to the monster is the one that any other inhabitant of the real world would have: they are terrified, disgusted, overwhelmed. To put it briefly, Kafka needs to set his unverisimilar story in a verisimilar background. If Gregor also found a talking wolf in his bedroom and together they decided to go off to a Mad Hatter's tea party, we would have another story (although this, too, would have many aspects of the real world as background).

But let's try to imagine a world even more unverisimilar than Kafka's. Edwin Abbott, in his novel *Flatland*, has conceived of such a world, which he presents to us in the words of one of its inhabitants, in his first chapter, "Of the Nature of Flatland":[3]

> Imagine a vast sheet of paper on which straight Lines, Triangles, Squares, Pentagons, Hexagons, and other figures, instead of remaining fixed in their places, move freely about, on or in the surface, but without the power of rising above or sinking below

it, very much like shadows—only hard and with luminous edges—and you will then have a pretty correct notion of my country and countrymen.

If we looked at this two-dimensional world from above, as we look at the figures of Euclid in a geometry book, we would be able to recognize its inhabitants. But for the dwellers in Flatland, the notion of "above" doesn't exist, because it's a concept that requires the third dimension. So the Flatlanders can't recognize one another by sight.

> We could see nothing of the kind, not at least so as to distinguish one figure from another. Nothing was visible, nor could be visible, to us, except Straight Lines.

In case the reader finds this situation unlikely, Abbott is quick to point out how possible it is in terms of our experience of the real world:

> When I was in Spaceland I heard that your sailors have very similar experiences while they traverse your seas and discern some distant island or coast lying on the horizon. The far-off land may have bays, forelands, angles in and out to any number and extent; yet at a distance you see none of these . . . , nothing but a grey unbroken line upon the water.

From an apparently impossible fact, Abbott deduces the conditions of possibility by making an analogy to what is possible in the real world. And since for the Flatlanders differences in shape mean differences of sex or of caste, and since they therefore have to know how to distinguish a triangle from a pentagon, Abbott shows, with great ingenuity, how it is possible for the lower classes to recognize the others by voice or touch (Chapter 5: "Of Our Methods of Recognising One Another"), while the upper classes can make such distinctions by sight, thanks to a providential feature of that world—namely, that it is always blanketed by fog. Here then, as in Nerval, fog plays an important role—although this time it's not an effect of the discourse but a "real" feature of the story.

> If Fog were non-existent, all lines would appear equally and indistinguishably clear . . . But wherever there is a rich supply of Fog objects that are at a distance, say of three feet, are appreciably dimmer than those at a distance of two feet eleven inches; and the result is that by careful and constant experimental observation of comparative dimness and clearness, we are enabled to infer with great exactness the configuration of the object observed. (Chapter 6: "Of Recognition by Sight")

To render the proceedings more probable, Abbott presents various regular figures, with a great show of exact geometrical calculation. He thus explains, for example, that when we meet a triangle in Flatland, we naturally apprehend its top angle as very bright because it is nearer to the observer, while on either side the lines will fade away rapidly into dimness because the two sides recede into the fog. We have to summon all our knowledge of geometry acquired in the real world to render this unreal world possible.

We could say that, however improbable, Abbott's world *is* nevertheless geometrically or perceptually possible—just as in reality it is possible that, through an accident in the evolution of the species, once upon a time there were wolves with certain phonatory organs or brain characteristics that allowed them to speak.

But as critics have shown, there are such things as "self-voiding" fictions—that is, fictional texts that demonstrate their own impossibility. According to a beautiful analysis by Lubomir Doležel, in these worlds, as in *Flatland,* an author can bring possible entities into fictional existence by applying "conventional authentication procedures"; yet "the status of this existence is made dubious because the very foundation of the authenticating mechanism is undermined." Doležel quotes, for instance, Robbe-Grillet's *La Maison de rendez-vous (The House of Assignation)*, which appears to be an impossible world because "a) one and the same event is introduced in several conflicting versions; b) one and the same place (Hong-Kong) is and is not the setting of the novel; c) events are ordered in contradictory temporal sequences (A precedes B, B precedes A); d) one and the same fictional entity recurs in several existential modes (as fictional 'reality' or theater performance or sculpture or painting etc.)."[4]

Certain authors[5] have suggested that a good visual metaphor of a self-voiding fiction is the celebrated optical illusion shown in Figure 11, which on a first "reading" gives both the impression of a coherent world and the feeling of some inexplicable impos-

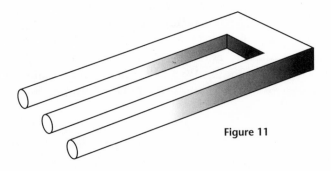

Figure 11

sibility. On a second reading (to read it properly, one should try to design it), one realizes how and why it is bidimensionally possible but tridimensionally absurd.

Yet even in this case, the impossibility of a universe in which Figure 11 can exist derives from the fact that we tend to think such a universe operates according to the same laws of solid geometry that obtain in the real world. Obviously, if these laws hold, the figure is impossible. But as a matter of fact, this figure is not geometrically impossible, and the proof is that it was possible to design it on a bidimensional surface. We are simply misled when we apply to it not only the rules of plane geometry but also the rules of perspective used in drawing three-dimensional objects. This figure would be possible not only in Flatland but also in our own world, if we did not take the shading as a representation of shadows on a three-dimensional structure. And so we must admit that in order to be impressed, disturbed, frightened, or touched by even the most impossible of worlds, we must rely upon our knowledge of the actual one. In other words, we ought to take the real world as background.

This means that fictional worlds are parasites of the real world. There is no rule that prescribes the number of fictional elements that are acceptable in a work. In fact, there is a great deal of variety here—forms such as the fable, for instance, lead us to accept correctives to our knowledge of the real world at every step. But everything that the text doesn't name or describe explicitly as different from what exists in the real world must be understood as corresponding to the laws and conditions of the real world.

Earlier in these lectures I cited two fictional passages in which there was a horse and a carriage. The first one, by Achille Campanile, made us laugh because the character Gedeone, asking a coachman to come and pick him up the next day, specified that he ought to bring the coach as well—and by the way, "Don't forget the horse!" We laughed because it seemed obvious that the horse had to come too, even if it hadn't been mentioned explicitly. We encountered another coach in *Sylvie:* during the night, it takes our narrator toward Loisy. If you read the pages where that journey is described (but you can trust me on this score), you will see that the horse is never mentioned. So maybe that horse doesn't exist in *Sylvie,* since it doesn't appear in the text? Yet it does exist. While reading, you imagine it trotting through the night, imparting a bumping movement to the carriage, and it is under the physical influence of those soft bumps that the narrator, as if listening to a lullaby, begins once more to dream.

But let us suppose we are not very imaginative readers: we read Nerval, and we don't think about the horse. Now let us suppose that, once he had arrived at Loisy, the narrator had told us: "I stepped out of the coach and I found that throughout the whole journey from Paris it had not been drawn by a horse." Sensitive readers would no doubt start and would hurry back to read the book from the beginning, because they had settled into a story of delicate and scarcely definable feelings in the best romantic spirit, whereas they should instead have been settling into a Gothic novel. Or perhaps they were reading a romantic variation of Cinderella, and the carriage was actually drawn by mice.

To sum up, there *is* a horse in *Sylvie*. It exists in the sense that it is not necessary to say there is one, but you can't say there *isn't* one.

Rex Stout's detective stories take place in New York City, and his readers agree to pretend that characters called Nero Wolfe, Archie Goodwin, Fritz, and Saul Panzer exist; in fact, readers even accept that Wolfe lives in a sandstone house on West Thirty-fifth Street, near the Hudson River. They could go to New York and see if it really exists, or if it existed in the years in which Stout sets his tales; but they usually don't bother. I say "usually" because we all know that there are people who go looking for Sherlock Holmes's house in Baker Street, and I happen to be one of those who has gone looking for the house in Eccles Street in Dublin where Leopold Bloom is supposed to have lived. But these are episodes of literary fanship—which is a pleasant activity, and moving at times, but different from the reading of texts. To be a good reader of Joyce, it's not necessary to celebrate Bloomsday on the banks of the Liffey.

But although we accept that Wolfe's house is where it wasn't and isn't, we couldn't accept that Archie Goodwin hails a taxi on Fifth Avenue and asks to be taken to Alexanderplatz—because, as Döblin has taught us, Alexanderplatz is in Berlin. And if Archie were to leave Nero Wolfe's home (on West Thirty-fifth Street), turn the corner, and find himself straightaway on Wall Street, we would be justified in believing that Stout had gone over to a different kind of fiction and wanted to tell us of a world analogous to that of Kafka's *The Trial*, where K goes into a building at one point in the city and comes out from the building at another. But in Kafka's story we must accept that we are moving in a non-Euclidean world, mobile and elastic, as if we were living on an immense piece of chewed chewing gum.

Thus, it seems that readers have to know a lot of things about the actual world in order to take it as the correct background of the fictional one. But at this point we face a predicament. On the one hand, insofar as it tells us the story of only a few characters, usually in a well-defined time and place, a fictional universe can be seen as a small world infinitely more limited than the actual one. On the other hand, insofar as it adds some individuals, properties, and events to the whole of the actual universe (which serves as its background), it can be considered greater than the world of our experience. From this point of view, a fictional universe doesn't end with the story itself but extends indefinitely.

In reality, fictional worlds *are* parasites of the actual one, but they are in effect "small worlds" which bracket most of our competence of the actual world and allow us to concentrate on a finite, enclosed world, very similar to ours but ontologically poorer. Since we cannot wander outside its boundaries, we are led to explore it in depth. It is for this reason that *Sylvie* is such a magical work. It indeed requires that we know and pretend to know something about Paris and the Valois, and even about Rousseau and the Medici, because it names them; yet it demands that we walk in that limited world over and over again without wondering about the rest of the actual world. In reading *Sylvie* we cannot deny that there is a horse, but we are not requested to know everything about horses. On the contrary, we are obliged to muse over and over again about the woods of Loisy.

In an essay published long ago, I wrote that we know Julien Sorel (the main character of Stendhal's *Le Rouge et le noir*) better than our own father.[6] Many aspects of our father will always escape us (thoughts he kept quiet about, actions apparently un-explained, unspoken affections, secrets kept hidden, memories and events of his childhood), whereas we know everything about Julien that there is to know. When I wrote that essay, my father was still alive. Since then I've realized how much more I would have liked to know about him, and I'm left to draw feeble conclusions from lackluster memories. Stendhal, however, tells me everything about Julien Sorel and about his generation that I need to know for the purposes of this novel. What I'm not told about (for example, whether he liked his first toy, or—as in Proust—whether he tossed and turned in his bed while waiting for his mother's goodnight kiss) is not important.

(By the way, it can also happen that a narrator tells us too much—that is, tells us what is irrelevant to the course of the story. At the start of my first lecture, I ironically quoted poor Carolina Invernizio because she once wrote that at the Turin railway station "two nonstop trains were meeting, one about to leave, the other about to arrive." Her description appeared to be a silly case of redundancy. But on second thought, I must confess that this piece of information is not as redundant as it seems. Where is it that two trains that meet do not both leave immediately after arriving? In a terminal station. Carolina was implicitly informing us that the Turin railway station was a terminus, as in fact it still is. Yet the reason we are entitled to consider her remark, if not semantically redundant, at least narratively useless, is that such a detail is simply not essential to the development of the story: the events that follow do not depend on the characteristics of the Turin station.)

I mentioned at the beginning of this lecture a reader who checked in the newspapers of the actual Paris and who discovered a fire that my book did not mention. He did not accept the idea that a fictional world has a more modest format than the actual world. Now let me tell you another story concerning that same night in June 1984.

Two students from the Ecole des Beaux Arts in Paris recently came to show me a photograph album in which they had reconstructed the entire route taken by my character Casaubon, having photographed, at the same time of night, each of the places I had mentioned. Since the text describes in detail how Casaubon comes up out of the city drains and enters, through the cellar, an Oriental bar full of sweating customers, beer kegs, and greasy spits, they succeeded in finding the bar and took a photo of it. It goes without saying that that bar was an invention of mine, even though I designed it thinking of the many bars of that kind in the area, but those two students had undoubtedly discovered the bar described in my book. It's not that they had superimposed on their duty as model readers the concerns of the empirical reader who wants to verify that my novel describes the real Paris. On the contrary, they wanted to transform the "real" Paris into a place in my book, and of all that they could have found in Paris, they chose only those aspects that corresponded to my descriptions.

They used a novel to give form to that shapeless and immense universe which the real Paris is. They did exactly the contrary of what Georges Perec did when he tried to represent everything that happened in the place Saint-Sulpice in the course of two days. Paris is far more complex than the locale described by Perec and the one described in my book. But any walk within fictional worlds has the same function as a child's play. Children play with puppets, toy horses, or kites in order to get acquainted with the physical laws of the universe and with the actions that someday they will really perform. Likewise, to read fiction means to play a game by which we give sense to the immensity of things that happened, are happening, or will happen in the actual world. By reading narrative, we escape the anxiety that attacks us when we try to say something true about the world.

This is the consoling function of narrative—the reason people tell stories, and have told stories from the beginning of time. And it has always been the paramount function of myth: to find a shape, a form, in the turmoil of human experience.

Nevertheless, the situation is not so simple. Until now my talk has been haunted by the ghost of Truth, and you must admit that this is not a notion to be taken lightly. Usually we think we know pretty well what it means when we say that something is "true" in the actual world. It is true that today is Wednesday, it is true that Alexanderplatz is in Berlin, it is true that Napoleon died May 5, 1821. On the basis of such a concept of truth, scholars have widely discussed what it means for an assertion to be "true" in a fictional framework. The most reasonable answer is that fictional statements are true within the framework of the possible world of a given story. We assume it is untrue that Hamlet lived in the actual world. But let us say we are grading the term paper of an undergraduate majoring in English literature and we find the wretched student has written that at the end of the tragedy Hamlet marries Ophelia. I bet that any reasonable teacher would claim the student has said something untrue. The statement would be untrue in the fictional universe of Hamlet, just as it is true in the fictional universe of *Gone with the Wind* that Scarlett O'Hara marries Rhett Butler.

Are we sure that our notion of truth in the actual world is equally strong and clear cut?

We think we usually know the real world through experience; we think it is a matter of experience that today is Wednesday, April 14, 1993, and that at this moment I'm wearing a blue tie. As a matter of fact, it is true that today is April 14, 1993, only within the framework of the Gregorian calendar, and my tie is blue only according to the Western division of the chromatic spectrum (it is well known that in the Latin and Greek cultures the boundaries between green and blue were different from the ones that obtain in our own culture). At Harvard, one can ask Willard Van Orman Quine to what extent our notions of truth are determined by a given holistic system of assumptions, Nelson Goodman about our many different ways of worldmaking, and Thomas Kuhn about the notion of truth with respect to a given scientific paradigm. I hope they would admit that it is true Scarlett married Rhett only in the universe of discourse of *Gone with the Wind,* just as it is true I am wearing a blue tie only in the universe of discourse of a given *Farbenlehre.*

I do not want to play the role either of a metaphysical skeptic or of a solipsist (it has been suggested that the world is overpopulated with solipsists). I realize there are things we know via direct experience, and if one of you told me that an armadillo had appeared behind me, I would turn around instantly to see whether the information was true or false. I think we can all agree that there are no armadillos in this room (provided we agree on the socially accepted zoological taxonomy). But usually our struggle with the notions of truth and falsity is more complicated than that. We know now that there are no armadillos in this room, but in the coming hours and days such a truth will become a little more arguable. For instance, when these lectures of mine are published, readers will accept the idea that on April 14, 1993, there weren't any armadillos in this room and will do so not on the basis of their own experience, but on the basis of their conviction that I am a serious person and that I have accurately reported the situation in this room on April 14, 1993.

We believe that, so far as the actual world is concerned, truth is the most important criterion, whereas we tend to think that fiction describes a world we have to take as it is, on trust. Even in the actual world, however, the principle of trust is as important as the principle of truth.

I don't know through experience that Napoleon died in 1821. Moreover, if I had to depend on my own experience I couldn't even say that Napoleon ever existed (as a matter of fact, somebody once wrote a book to demonstrate that Napoleon was a Solar Myth). I don't know through experience that there is a city called Hong Kong, and I don't even know through experience that the first atomic bomb worked by fission and not by fusion; I actually don't know very much about how atomic fusion works. According to Hilary Putnam, there is a "linguistic division of labor" which corresponds to a social division of knowledge: I delegate to others the knowledge of nine-tenths of the real world, keeping for myself the knowledge of the other tenth.[7] In two months I really will be going to Hong Kong; I'll buy my ticket certain that the plane is going to land in a place called

Hong Kong, and I'll thereby manage to live in the real world without having to behave neurotically. I've learned that for a lot of things, I've been used to putting my faith in other people's knowledge. I confine my doubts to some specialized sector of knowledge, and for the rest I put my trust in the Encyclopedia. By "Encyclopedia" I mean the totality of knowledge, with which I'm only partly acquainted but to which I can refer because it is like an enormous library composed of all books and encyclopedias—all the papers and manuscript documents of all centuries, including the hieroglyphics of the ancient Egyptians and inscriptions in cuneiform.

Experience, and a long series of decisions by which I have placed trust in the human community, have convinced me that what the Total Encyclopedia describes (quite often in contradictory ways) represents a satisfactory image of what I call the real world. In other words, the way we accept the representation of the actual world scarcely differs from the way we accept the representation of fictional worlds. I pretend to believe that Scarlett married Rhett, just as I pretend to take as a matter of personal experience that Napoleon married Josephine. Obviously the difference lies in the degree of this trust: the trust I give Margaret Mitchell is different from the trust I give historians. Only when I read a fable do I accept that wolves speak; the rest of the time I behave as if the wolves in question are those described by the latest International Congress of the Zoological Society. I do not want to discuss here the reasons I put more trust in the Zoological Society than in Charles Perrault. These reasons exist and are pretty serious. But to say that these reasons are serious does not mean that they can be clearly spelled out. On the contrary, the reasons for which I believe historians when they tell me that Napoleon died in 1821 are far more complex than the reasons for which I am sure that Scarlett O'Hara married Rhett Butler.

In *The Three Musketeers* we read that Lord Buckingham was stabbed by one of his officers, called Felton, and so far as I know this is considered a historical truth; in *Twenty Years Later* we read that Athos stabbed Mordaunt, the son of Milady, and this is considered a fictional truth. That Athos stabbed Mordaunt will remain an undeniable truth so long as there exists a single copy of *Twenty Years Later*—even if in the future someone invents a post-post-structuralist way of reading. In contrast, a serious historian must remain ready to assert that Buckingham was stabbed by someone else, if by chance a future researcher in the British Archives proves that all previously known documents are false. In such a case we would say that it is historically untrue that Felton stabbed Buckingham, but the same fact would remain fictionally true.

Apart from many important aesthetic reasons, I think that we read novels because they give us the comfortable sensation of living in worlds where the notion of truth is indisputable, while the actual world seems to be a more treacherous place. This "alethic privilege" of fictional worlds also provides us with some parameters for challenging farfetched interpretations of literary texts.

There have been many interpretations of "Little Red Riding Hood" (anthropological, psychoanalytical, mythological, feminist, and so on), in part because the story exists in several versions: in the Brothers Grimm text there are things that are not in Perrault's, and vice versa. It was reasonable to expect an alchemical interpretation, as well. In fact, an Italian scholar has tried to prove that the fable refers to the processes of extracting and treating minerals. Translating the fable into chemical formulas, he has identified Little Red Riding Hood as cinnabar, an artificial mercury sulfide which is as red as her hood is supposed to be. Thus, within herself, the child contains mercury in its pure state, which has to be separated from the sulphur. Mercury is very lively and mobile, and it is no accident that Little Red Riding Hood's mother warns her not to go poking about everywhere. The wolf stands for mercurous chloride, otherwise known as calomel (which means "beautiful black" in Greek). The stomach of the wolf is the alchemist's oven in which the cinnabar is transformed into mercury. Valentina Pisanty has made a very simple comment: if, at the end of the story, Little Red Riding Hood is no longer cinnabar but mercury in its pure state, how can it be that when she steps out of the wolf's belly she's still wearing a red hood? There is no version of the fable in which the little girl steps out wearing a silver hood. So the fable doesn't support this interpretation.[8]

You may infer from texts things they don't explicitly say—and the collaboration of the reader is based on this principle—but you can't make them say the contrary of what they have said. You can't ignore the fact that Little Red Riding Hood at the end is still wearing her red hood: it is precisely this textual fact that exempts the model reader from being obliged to know the chemical formula for cinnabar.

Can we rely on the same degree of certainty when we speak of truth in the actual world? We are sure that there are no armadillos in this room to at least the same extent we are sure that Scarlett O'Hara married Rhett Butler. But for many other truths we must rely on the good faith of our informers, and sometimes on their bad faith. In epistemological terms, we cannot be sure that Americans landed on the moon (whereas we are sure that Flash Gordon reached the planet Mongo). Let's for a moment be extremely skeptical (and mildly paranoid): it could have happened that a small bunch of conspirators (say, people from the Pentagon and various TV channels) organized a Big Fake. We—I mean, all other TV watchers—simply trusted those images telling us that a man had landed on the moon.

There is, however, a strong reason that makes me believe Americans really did reach the moon: it is the fact that the Russians did not protest and did not make any accusations of fakery. They had the ability to prove that it was a hoax and they had every good reason to do so. They did not. I trusted them, so I strongly believe that Americans reached the moon. But in order to decide what is true or false in the actual world, I must make some difficult decisions about my trust in the community. Furthermore, I must decide which portions of the Total Encyclopedia are to be trusted, while rejecting others as unreliable.

It seems that with fictional truths things go easier. Even a fictional world can be as treacherous as the actual one, however. It would be a wholly comfortable environment if it had to deal only with fictional entities and events. In that case, nobody would have any anxious moments over Scarlett O'Hara, because the fact that she lived at Tara is easier to check than the fact that Americans landed on the moon.

But we have ascertained that every fictional world is based, parasitically, upon the actual one, which the fictional world takes as its background. We can skip a first question—namely, what happens when the reader brings into the fictional world wrong information about the actual world. We can assume that such a reader does not behave like a model one, and the consequences of this remain a private and empirical affair. If someone reads *War and Peace* believing that in the nineteenth century Russians were governed by the Communist party, it will be hard for him or her to understand the story of Natasha and Pierre Besuchov.

I have said, though, that the profile of the model reader is designed by and within the text. Obviously Tolstoy did not feel obliged to inform his readers that the battle of Borodino wasn't fought by the Red Army, but he provided his readers with enough information about the political and social situation of czarist Russia in that period. Don't forget that his novel opens with a long dialogue in French, and this tells the reader a lot about the situation of the Russian aristocracy at the beginning of the nineteenth century.

In fact, not only are authors supposed to take the actual world as the background of their story, but they constantly intervene to inform their readers about various aspects of the actual world they may not know.

Suppose that Rex Stout in one of his novels were to say that Archie, hailing a cab, asks the driver to take him to the corner of Fourth and Tenth Streets. Suppose further that Rex Stout's readers fall into two categories, those who do not know New York and those who do. Let's disregard the first category—they are eager to swallow everything (in Italian translations of American detective novels, such expressions as "downtown" and "uptown" are regularly translated as "città alta" and "città bassa"—"high city" and "low city"—so that most Italian readers think American cities are all like Tiflis, Bergamo, or Budapest, half on the hills and half on the plain or along the river). But I think that most American readers, knowing that New York City is like a world map where the streets are the parallels and the avenues are the meridians, would react like that reader to whom a hypothetical Nerval said that the coach was not drawn by a horse. As a matter of fact, there is in New York (in the West Village) a point where Fourth Street and Tenth Street intersect, and all New Yorkers know it, except the taxi drivers. I believe, however, that if Stout had had to narrate this event, he would have explained this fact (maybe by inserting an amusing comment) and the reason this intersection can really exist, being afraid that a reader from San Francisco, Rome, or Madrid might not be aware of this and might think that Stout was joking.

He would have done it for the same reason that Walter Scott began *Ivanhoe* like this:

> In that pleasant district of merry England which is watered by the river Don, there extended in ancient times a large forest, covering the greatest part of the beautiful hills and valleys which lie between Sheffield and the pleasant town of Doncaster.

After supplying other historical details, he goes on:

> This state of things I have thought it necessary to premise for the information of the general reader.

Not only was Scott intent on coming to some sort of agreement with his reader about facts and events that occurred in the fiction; he also wanted to supply information about the real world which he was not sure his reader possessed and which he believed indispensable for understanding the story. His readers were thus supposed both to *pretend to believe* that the fictional information was true and to accept the additional information provided by the author as being true in the actual world.

At times, information is given to us in the form of that rhetorical figure known as *preterition.* Washington Irving's "Rip Van Winkle" begins, "Whoever has made a voyage up the Hudson must remember the Kaatskill Mountains . . . ," but I really don't believe that the book is aimed just at those people who have gone up the Hudson and seen the Catskill Mountains. I think I am a good example of a reader who has never been up the Hudson and yet has pretended to have been up it, has pretended to have seen those mountains, and has enjoyed the rest of the story. But my suspension of disbelief has been only partial. I know that Rip Van Winkle has never existed; nevertheless, I not only believe but I assume to know that up the Hudson River one can really find the Catskill Mountains.

In my essay "Small Worlds," now in *The Limits of Interpretation,* I quoted the beginning of Ann Radcliffe's novel *The Mysteries of Udolpho:*

> On the pleasant banks of the Garonne, in the province of Gascony, stood, in the year 1584, the château of Monsier St. Aubert. From its windows were seen the pastoral landscapes of Guienne and Gascony stretching along the river, gay with luxuriant woods and wine, and plantations of olives.

My comment was that it is doubtful whether English readers of the late eighteenth century would have known much about the Garonne, Gascony, and the corresponding landscape. At most, they would have been able to infer from the word "banks" that the Garonne was a river and would have imagined, on the basis of their knowledge of the actual world, a typical southern European environment with vines and olives. Radcliffe invited her readers to behave as if they were familiar with the hills of France.

After publishing that essay, I received a letter from a gentleman of Bordeaux, who revealed to me that olive trees have never grown in Gascony or on the banks of the Garonne. This amiable person drew witty conclusions to support my thesis and praised my ignorance of Gascony, which had allowed me to choose such a convincing example (he then invited me to visit the region as his guest because, he maintained, vineyards *did* exist there and the wines of that area are exquisite).

So not only did Ann Radcliffe ask her readers to collaborate with her on the basis of their competence concerning the actual world, and not only did she supply part of that competence, and not only did she ask them to pretend to know things about the real world that they did not know, but she even led them to believe that the real world was endowed with items which are not in fact part of its actual furnishings.

Since it is extremely unlikely that Mrs. Radcliffe intended to deceive her readers, we must conclude that she was wrong. But this creates an even greater conundrum. To what extent can we take for granted those aspects of the actual world that the author erroneously takes for granted?

THE STRANGE CASE OF THE RUE SERVANDONI

A recent dissertation by my student Lucrecia Escudero, concerning the Argentine press's coverage of the Falklands-Malvinas war, contained the following story.[1]

On March 31, 1982, two days before the Argentine landing in the Malvinas and twenty-five days before the arrival of the British Task Force in the Falklands, the Buenos Aires newspaper *Clarin* published an interesting item: allegedly, a London source claimed that Britain had sent the Superb, a nuclear submarine, to the Austral area of the South Atlantic. The British Foreign Office said immediately that they did not have any comment on this "version," and the Argentine press inferred that, if the British authorities qualified the report as a "version," this meant someone had leaked serious and secret military information. On April 1, when Argentines were on the verge of landing in the Malvinas, *Clarin* reported that the Superb was a ship of 45,000 tons, carrying a crew of ninety-seven specialists in scuba diving.

Subsequent reactions by the British were pretty ambiguous. A military expert said that sending atomic submarines of the hunter-killer type to that region would have been reasonable. The *Daily Telegraph* gave the impression of knowing a lot about the whole business, and step by step the rumor became fact.

Argentine readers were shocked by the event, and the press tried to meet their narrative expectations by keeping them in suspense. The information it gave allegedly came directly from the Argentine military command, and the Superb became "that submarine which English sources locate in the South Atlantic." On April 4 the submarine had already been sighted not far from the Argentine coasts. British military sources continued to answer all questions by saying they had no intention of revealing the location of their submarines, and such an obvious statement reinforced the general opinion that there were English submarines somewhere—which, of course, was quite true.

Also on April 4 several European press agencies reported that the Superb was on the verge of sailing toward the South Seas, at the head of the British Task Force. If this had been so, the submarine sighted near the Argentine coasts could not have been the Superb, but such a contradiction reinforced, rather than weakened, the submarine syndrome.

On April 5 the press agency DAN announced that the Superb was 250 kilometers from the Falklands-Malvinas. The rest of the media followed, describing all the characteristics of the submarine and its extraordinary power. On April 6 the Argentine navy spotted the vessel near the archipelago, and in the following week it was joined by a brother, the submarine Oracle. On April 8 the French daily *Le Monde* mentioned the two ships, and the *Clarin* quoted the French report under the dramatic title "A Submarine Fleet?" On April 12 the submarine fleet showed up again, and *Clarin* furthermore announced the arrival of Soviet submarines in southern waters.

Now, this story concerns not only the presence of the Superb (which was taken for granted) but also the diabolical abilities of the Britons, who succeeded in keeping their position secret. On April 18 a Brazilian pilot sighted the Superb near Santa Catarina and took a photograph of it, but the image was blurred because of the cloudy weather. Here is yet another effect of fog (the third one in these lectures, if you remember), this time provided directly by readers in order to sustain the necessary suspense of the story. We seem to be halfway between *Flatland* and Antonioni's *Blow Up.*

On April 22, when the British Task Force was really eighty kilometers from the theater of operations, with true warships and true submarines, *Clarin* informed its readers that the submarine which had allegedly been patrolling the Malvinas area had returned to Scotland. On April 23 the Scottish *Daily Record* revealed that, as a matter of fact, the Superb had never left its British base. Argentine newspapers were obliged to find another narrative genre, shifting from war movies to spy novels, and on April 23 *Clarin* announced triumphantly that the deception of the British forces had been unmasked.

Who invented that Yellow Submarine? The British secret services, in order to lower the spirits of Argentines? The Argentine military command, in order to justify its tough stance? The British press? The Argentine press? Who benefited from the rumor? I am not interested in this side of the story. I am interested in the way the whole story grew out of vague gossip, through the collaboration of all parties. Everybody cooperated in the creation of the Yellow Submarine because it was a fascinating fictional character and its story was narratively exciting.

This story—that is, the real story of a fictional construction—has many morals. In the first place, it shows that we are continually tempted to give shape to life through narrative schemes (but this will be the topic of my next and last lecture). Second, it demonstrates the force of existential presuppositions.[2] In every statement involving proper names or definite descriptions, the reader or listener is supposed to take for granted the existence of the entity about which something is predicated. If someone tells me that he was unable to attend a meeting because his wife was ill, my first reaction is to take for granted the existence of that wife. Only later, if by chance I discover that the speaker is a bachelor, can I conclude that he was lying through his teeth. But until that moment, because his wife has been *posited* within the discursive framework by the act of mentioning her, I have no reason to think she does not exist. This is such a natural inclination on the part of normal human beings that if I read a text beginning, "As everyone knows, the present king of France is bald" (taking into account that France is generally known to be a republic and that I am not a philosopher of language but a normal human being), I do not start consulting the Truth Tables; rather, I decide to suspend my disbelief and take that discourse as a fictional one, which probably tells a story set in the time of Charles the Bald. I do this because it is the only way to assign a form of existence in whatever world to the entity posited by the statement.

Thus it happened with our submarine. Once posited by the discourse of the mass media, the submarine was there, and since newspapers are supposed to tell the truth about the actual world, people did their best to sight it.

In *Ma che cos'è questo amore,* by Achille Campanile (that sublime comic writer I quoted in my first lecture), there is a character named Baron Manuel who, in order to facilitate his secret adulterous life, continually tells his wife and others that he is obliged to visit and assist a certain Pasotti, a dear friend of his, who is chronically ill and whose health tragically declines as Baron Manuel's love affairs become more and more complicated. The presence of Pasotti is so palpable in the novel that even though both the author and the reader know he does not exist, there comes a point where everybody (certainly the other characters, but also the reader) is prepared for him to appear physically on the scene. So Pasotti suddenly shows up, unfortunately a few minutes after Baron Manuel (who has become disgusted with his adulterous life) has announced Pasotti's death.

The Yellow Submarine was posited by the media, and as soon as it was posited everyone took it for granted. What happens when in a fictional text the author posits, as an element of the actual world (which is the background of the fictional one), something that does not obtain in the actual world? As you may remember, this is the case of Ann Radcliffe, who posited olive trees in Gascony.

In the first chapter of *The Three Musketeers*, d'Artagnan arrives in Paris and soon finds lodgings on the rue des Fossoyeurs, at the house of Monsieur Bonacieux. Monsieur de Tréville's residence, to which he goes immediately afterward, is on the rue du Vieux Colombier (Chapter 2). Only in the seventh chapter do we learn that Porthos lives on the same street and that Athos lives on the rue Férou. Today the rue du Vieux Colombier runs along the north side of the present place Saint-Sulpice, while the rue Férou joins it perpendicularly on the south side, but in the days in which *The Three Musketeers* is set the square did not yet exist. Where are the lodgings of that reticent and mysterious individual who goes by the name of Aramis? We find this out in Chapter 11, where we learn that he lives on a corner of the rue Servandoni, and if you look at a map of Paris (Figure 12) you'll notice that the rue Servandoni is the first street running parallel to and east of the rue Férou. This eleventh chapter is called "L'Intrigue se noue" ("The Plot Grows Tangled"). Though Dumas, of course, had something different in mind, for us the plot grows tangled from the point of view of onomastics and town planning.

One night, after visiting Monsieur de Tréville on the rue du Vieux Colombier, d'Artagnan (who is in no hurry to go home, wanting to take a walk so that he can think tenderly of his beloved, Madame Bonacieux) returns to his rooms by "the longest way round," as the text tells us. But we don't know where the rue des Fossoyeurs is, and if we look at a map of present-day Paris we won't find it. So let's follow d'Artagnan, who is "talking to the night and smiling at the stars" (see Figure 13).

If we read Dumas' text looking at a seventeenth-century map, we see that d'Artagnan turns down the rue du Cherche-Midi (which at that time, Dumas notes, was called Chasse-Midi), wends his way along a little street that lies where the rue d'Assas is today and that was undoubtedly the rue des Carmes, and then turns left "because Aramis' house was between the rue Cassette

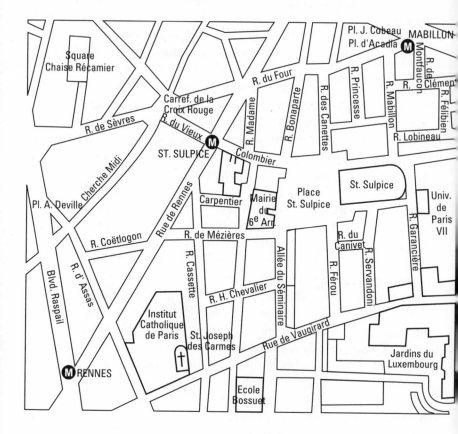

Figure 12

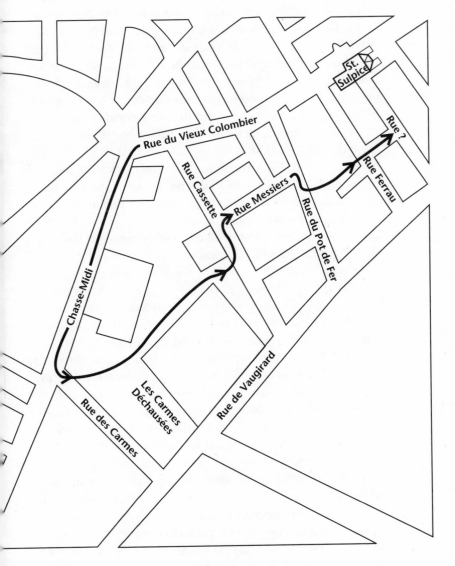

Figure 13

and the rue Servandoni." After leaving the rue des Carmes d'Artagnan probably cuts across some land next to the convent of the Barefooted Carmelites, makes a dogleg at the rue Cassette, enters the rue Messiers (now Mézières), and somehow crosses the rue Férou (in those days known as the rue Ferrau), where Athos lives, without even realizing it (but of course d'Artagnan is wandering along just as people in love tend to do). If Aramis' house lies between the rue Cassette and the rue Servandoni, it should be located on the rue du Canivet (though apparently the rue du Canivet didn't yet exist in 1625).[3] But it should be precisely on the corner of the rue Servandoni (on our map, "Rue?"), because just opposite his friend's house d'Artagnan sees a shadowy form leave the rue Servandoni (later in the novel we find out that this was Madame Bonacieux).

Alas, our empirical reader will certainly be moved at the mention of the rue Servandoni, because Roland Barthes lived there, but Aramis couldn't have, because the action takes place in 1625 whereas the Florentine architect Giovanni Niccolò Servandoni was born in 1695, designed the façade of Saint-Sulpice Church in 1733, and had the street dedicated to him only in 1806.

Although Dumas even knew that the rue du Cherche-Midi was then called Chasse-Midi, he was wrong when it came to the rue Servandoni. This wouldn't matter if the issue concerned only the empirical author Dumas. But now that the text exists, we obedient readers have to follow its instructions, and we find ourselves in an entirely real Paris, identical to the Paris of 1625, except that in the former a street appears which couldn't have existed.

As you know, logicians and philosophers of language have frequently debated the problem of the ontological status of fictional characters (as well as of fictional objects and events), and it is not preposterous to ask what it means to say that "p is true" when p is a proposition that refers not to the real world but to a fictional one. In the course of my previous lecture, however, we decided to stick to the most commonsensical opinion. Whatever your philosophical position, you would say that, in the fictional world of Conan Doyle, Sherlock Holmes is a bachelor; if in one of these stories Holmes were suddenly to tell Watson to book three train tickets because he is setting out with Mrs. Holmes to track down Dr. Moriarty, we would surely feel at the very least a little uneasy. Allow me to use a very crude notion of truth: it is not true that Holmes has a wife, just as it is not true that the Empire State Building is in Berlin. Period.

But can we really state with the same confidence that it is not true that Aramis lives on the corner of the rue Servandoni? Of course, we could argue that everything falls into place if we just say that in the possible world of *The Three Musketeers* Aramis lives on the corner of a certain X Street, and that only through the empirical author's error is this street called Servandoni, whereas in fact it was probably called something else. We have been persuaded by Keith Donnellan that if one believes and maintains by mistake that Jones is Smith's murderer, when one mentions Smith's murderer one definitely wants to indicate Jones, even if he's innocent.[4]

But the issue is more complicated than that. Where is the rue des Fossoyeurs, on which d'Artagnan lives? This street did exist in the seventeenth century, and doesn't now for a very simple reason: the old rue des Fossoyeurs was the one we now call the rue Servandoni. So (1) Aramis lives on a street which was not known by that name in 1625, and (2) d'Artagnan lives on the same street as Aramis without knowing it. Indeed d'Artagnan is in a pretty curious ontological situation: he believes that in his Paris of 1625 there are two streets with two different names, whereas there was only one with one name. We might say that an error of this kind is not unlikely. For many centuries humanity believed that off the southern coast of India there were two large islands, Ceylon and Taprobane, and sixteenth-century cartographers depicted them both; but subsequently it was learned that this doubling was the result of imaginative interpretation of the descriptions of various travelers, and that in reality there was only one island. Similarly, it was believed that the Morning Star was different from the Evening Star (Hesperus and Phosphorus, as they were called), but these are really the same celestial body—namely, Venus.

Nevertheless, this is not quite the same as d'Artagnan's situation. We earthly beings watch two entities, Hesperus and Phosphorus, from afar, at two different times of day, and it is understandable that we committed or still commit the mistake of believing they are two different entities. But if we were inhabitants of Phosphorus we couldn't possibly believe in the existence of Hesperus, because no one would ever have seen it shining in the sky. The problem of Hesperus and Phosphorus has preoccupied Frege and other terrestrial philosophers but does not exist for Phosphoric philosophers, if there are any. As an empirical author who has evidently made a mistake, Dumas is in the same situation as terrestrial philosophers. But d'Artagnan, in his possible world, is in the situation of Phosphoric philosophers. If he is on the street that today we call Servandoni, he must know that he is on the rue des Fossoyeurs, the street on which he lives. So how can he think that it is another street, the one on which Aramis lives?

If *The Three Musketeers* were a sci-fi novel (or an example of self-voiding fiction), there wouldn't be a problem. I could easily write the story of a space navigator who leaves Hesperus on January 1, 2001, and reaches Phosphorus on January 1, 1999. My story could posit the existence of parallel worlds in which there is a time gap of two years. One of these planets is called Hesperus; it has a million inhabitants and a king named Stan Laurel. The other is Phosphorus; its inhabitants number a million minus one (Stan Laurel doesn't exist on Phosphorus, which is a republic) and are exactly the same as those of Hesperus (same names, same characteristics, same individual histories, same family relationships). Or else I could imagine that the space navigator travels backward in time and reaches a past Hesperus, when it was still called Phosphorus, just half an hour before its inhabitants decide to change its name.

But one of the basic fictional agreements of every historical novel is that however many imaginary characters are introduced in the story, everything else has to more or less correspond to what happened in that era in the real world.

One good solution of our conundrum could be the following: Since according to some maps it appears that, at least about 1636, the rue des Fossoyeurs, after a certain point southward, was named the rue du Pied de Biche, then d'Artagnan lives on the rue des Fossoyeurs and Aramis on the rue du Pied de Biche. D'Artagnan, who thinks the two streets are different because they have different names, knows he lives on a street which is the continuation of Aramis' street, and by mere error believes that Aramis' street is called the rue Servandoni instead of the rue du Pied de Biche. Why not? Perhaps he has met a Florentine called Servandoni, great-grandfather of the architect of Saint-Sulpice, and his memory has pulled a fast one on him.

But the text doesn't tell us that d'Artagnan arrives at what "he believes" is the rue Servandoni. The text tells us that he arrives at what the *reader* should believe is the rue Servandoni. How can we resolve this most perplexing situation? By accepting the idea that up to now I have been caricaturing discussions about the ontology of fictional characters. What actually interests us is not the ontology of possible worlds and their inhabitants (a respectable problem in discussions of modal logic) but *the position of the reader.*

That Holmes isn't married we know from the Holmes saga—that is, from a fictional corpus. In contrast, that the rue Servandoni couldn't have existed in 1625 we can learn only from the Encyclopedia; and the Encyclopedia's information is, from the point of view of the textual world, irrelevant gossip. If you think about it for a moment, it's the same sort of problem that was posed by the wolf in "Little Red Riding Hood." We know very well as empirical readers that wolves don't speak, but as model readers we have to agree to live in a world where wolves do speak. So if we accept that there are speaking wolves in the wood, why can't we accept that there was a rue Servandoni in Paris in 1625? And in reality that's what we do and what you will continue to do if you reread *The Three Musketeers,* even after my revelations.

In my books *The Limits of Interpretation* and *Interpretation and Overinterpretation,* I insisted on the difference between *interpreting* a text and *using* a text, but I said that it is not forbidden to use a text for daydreaming. In this lecture I have "used" *The Three Musketeers* to allow myself an exciting adventure in the world of history and erudition. I must admit that I very much enjoyed walking the streets of Paris to find the ones named by Dumas and examining seventeenth-century plans of the city (all very inaccurate, by the way). You can do what you like with a fictional text. I enjoyed playing the role of paranoid reader and of checking to see whether seventeenth-century Paris corresponded to Dumas' descriptions.

But in doing this I did not behave like a model reader, or even like a normal empirical reader. To know who Servandoni was you have to know a lot about art, and to know that the rue des Fossoyeurs was the rue Servandoni you have to have a great deal of specialized knowledge. Dumas' text, which presents itself via stylistic signals as a popular historical novel, can't claim to have such a sophisticated sort of reader. So Dumas' model readers are not supposed to know this irrelevant detail—that in 1625 the rue Servandoni was called the rue des Fossoyeurs—and can carry on happily with their reading.

Does this solve everything? By no means. Let us imagine that Dumas had made d'Artagnan leave the Tréville residence in the rue du Vieux Colombier and had made him turn through the rue Bonaparte (which already existed at that time: it was perpendicular to the rue du Vieux Colombier and parallel to the rue Férou, and in those days was called the rue du Pot de Fer). Well, no, this would be too much. Either we would throw away the book indignantly or else we would try rereading it, convinced we had made a mistake in setting ourselves up as model readers of a historical novel. We would be dealing not with a historical novel, apparently, but with one of those stories that are called uchronian—that take place in a historical time all upside down, where Julius Caesar fights a duel with Napoleon, and Euclid finally manages to demonstrate Fermat's theorem.

Why can't we accept that d'Artagnan walks up the rue Bonaparte, whereas we can accept that he walks up the rue Servandoni? It's obvious: because almost everyone knows that it was impossible for the rue Bonaparte to have existed in the seventeenth century, while almost no one knows that the rue Servandoni couldn't have existed; not even Dumas knew that.

So our problem doesn't concern the ontology of the characters who live in fictional worlds, so much as the format of the model reader's Encyclopedia. The model readers foreseen by *The Three Musketeers* are quite keen on historical reconstruction (so long as it's not too scholarly) and know who Bonaparte was; they have only a vague idea of the difference between the reigns of Louis XIII and Louis XIV, so that the author supplies them with a lot of information both at the outset and during the story, and they do not intend to forage in the French national archives to see if there really was a Count de Rochefort in those days. Should they also know that at that time America had already been discovered? The text neither says so nor implies it, but it's reasonable to suppose that if d'Artagnan were to meet Christopher Columbus in the rue Servandoni, the reader should be amazed. "Should be," because I'm only supposing. There are readers who are certainly ready to believe that Columbus was a contemporary of d'Artagnan, because there are readers for whom everything that is not present is "past," and for them the past may be very vague indeed. So once we've said that the text presupposes a reader's Encyclopedia of a certain format, it's quite hard to ascertain what that format should be.

The first example that comes to mind is *Finnegans Wake*, which foresees, demands, and requires a model reader endowed with an infinite encyclopedic competence, superior to that of the empirical author James Joyce—a reader able to discover allusions and semantic connections even where they escaped the notice of the empirical author. In fact the text presupposes (as Joyce said) an "ideal reader affected by an ideal insomnia." Dumas didn't expect—would, on the contrary, have been irritated by—a reader like me, who checks to see where the rue des Fossoyeurs was. Joyce, on the other hand (even though the wood in *Finnegans Wake* is potentially infinite, so that once you're in you can't get out), wanted a reader who was able at any time to leave the wood and think of other woods, of the infinite forest of universal culture and *intertextuality*.

Can we say that every fictional text designs such a model reader, so similar to Borges' "Funes the Memorious"? Certainly not. The readers of "Little Red Riding Hood" are not supposed to know about Giordano Bruno, as the readers of *Finnegans Wake* certainly are. So, what is the format of the Encyclopedia that a "normal" narrative work requires of us?

Roger Schank and Peter Childers, in their book *The Cognitive Computer*, allow us to approach the problem from another point of view: What is the format of the Encyclopedia one should give to a machine so that it may write (and understand) Aesop-like fables?[5]

In their program Tale-Spin, they first started with a small-scale Encyclopedia: the computer was told how—given a set of problematic situations—a bear might plan to get some honey.

At the beginning of the computer trials, Joe Bear asked Irving Bird where he could find some honey, and Irving replied that "there was a beehive in the oak tree." But in one of the early stories generated by the computer, Joe Bear became miffed because he thought Irving hadn't answered him. In fact, his encyclopedic competence lacked the information that at times you can indicate the location of food by using metonymy—that is, by naming the source instead of the food itself. Proust praised Flaubert for writing that Madame Bovary drew near the fireplace and for considering it unnecessary to tell his readers that she was cold. Moreover, Flaubert took it for granted that his readers would know a fireplace produces warmth. In contrast, Schank and Childers realized that they had to be more explicit with a computer, and they supplied it with information on the relationship of food to its source. But when Irving Bird repeated that there was a beehive in the oak tree, Joe Bear walked over to the oak tree and ate the whole beehive. His Encyclopedia was still incomplete: the difference between source as a container and source as an object still had to be explained to him, because "finding a refrigerator will do when you are hungry [only] if you know you have to look inside it, and not eat it. None of this is obvious to a machine."[6]

Another unforeseen incident occurred when the machine was told how to use certain means to obtain certain ends (for example, "if a character wants some object, then one option he has is to try bargaining with the object's owner"). And so this happened:

Joe Bear was hungry. He asked Irving Bird where some honey was. Irving refused to tell him, so Joe offered to bring him a worm if he'd tell him where some honey was. Irving agreed. But Joe didn't know where any worms were, so he asked Irving, who refused to say. So Joe offered to bring him a worm if he'd tell him where a worm was. Irving agreed. But Joe didn't know where any worms were, so he asked Irving, who refused to say. So he offered to bring him a worm if he'd tell him where a worm was . . .[7]

To avoid this loop, the computer had to be told "not to give a character a goal if he already has it [that is, if he's already attempted it without success] but to try something else." But even these instructions caused problems, because they interacted badly with later information—for example, "If a character is hungry and sees some food, he will want to eat it. If a character is trying to get some food and fails, he will get sick from the lack of food."

Here is a story that the computer came up with. Bill Fox saw

Henry Crow sitting on a branch and holding a piece of cheese in his mouth. Bill was hungry and obviously wanted to eat the cheese, so he persuaded Henry Crow to sing. Henry opened his mouth and the cheese fell to the ground. Once the cheese was on the ground, Bill saw it again and should, under normal circumstances, have wanted to eat it. But the computer had been instructed not to give a character the same goal twice, so Bill could not satisfy his hunger and got sick. Too bad for Bill. But what happened to Henry Crow?

> Henry Crow saw the cheese on the ground, and he became hungry, but he knew that he owned the cheese. He felt pretty honest with himself, so he decided not to trick himself into giving up the cheese. He wasn't trying to deceive himself, either, nor did he feel competitive with himself, but he remembered that he was also in a position of dominance over himself, so he refused to give himself the cheese. He couldn't think of a good reason why he should give himself the cheese [if he did that, he'd lose the cheese], so he offered to bring himself a worm if he'd give himself the cheese. That sounded okay, but he didn't know where any worms were. So he said to himself, "Henry, do you know where any worms are?" But of course, he didn't, so he . . . [and so on].[8]

You really have to know a lot to read a fable. But however much Schank and Childers had to teach their computer, they didn't have to tell it where the rue Servandoni was. The world of Joe Bear was always a small world.

In order to read a work of fiction, one must have some notion of the economic criteria that rule the fictional world. The criteria aren't there—or rather, as in every hermeneutic circle, they have to be presupposed even as you are trying to infer them from the evidence of the text. For this reason, reading is like a bet. You bet that you will be faithful to the suggestions of a voice that is not saying explicitly what it is suggesting.

Let's return to Dumas and try reading him as if we were readers brought up on *Finnegans Wake*—that is, as if we were authorized to find evidence and clues all over the place for allusions and semantic short-circuits. Let's try to overinterpret *The Three Musketeers*.

One could suppose that naming the rue Servandoni was not a mistake but a trace, an allusion—that Dumas dropped this name in the margins of the text in order to alert his readers. He wanted them to realize that every fictional text contains a basic contradiction just because it's trying so hard to make the fictional world coincide with the real one. Dumas wanted to demonstrate that every fiction is a self-voiding fiction. The title of the chapter "The Plot Grows Tangled" refers not only to the love affairs of d'Artagnan or of the queen but to the nature of narrativity itself.

Here, however, the economic criteria come into play. We said that Nerval wanted us to reconstruct his story, and we could say this because the text of *Sylvie* contains an abundance of temporal signals. It is difficult to believe that those signals are fortuitous; it could scarcely be an accident that the only precise date in the novel comes right at the end, as if we were being invited to reread the novella to rediscover the sequence of the story, which the narrator has lost and we have not yet found. But the temporal signals scattered throughout Nerval's text all come at crucial moments in the plot, just when the reader feels lost. Those signals function like dim yet perceptible traffic lights at a foggy crossroads. On the other hand, anyone hunting for anachronisms in Dumas would perhaps find a good many, but none of them in very strategic places. In Chapter 11 the narrating voice focuses on the jealousy d'Artagnan is feeling, a drama that wouldn't have been altered no matter what route he followed as he walked. True, one might observe that the whole chapter revolves around a confusion of identities: first we see a shadow, then this is identified as Madame Bonacieux, then she speaks to someone d'Artagnan believes is Aramis, then we discover that that someone was a woman, at the end of the chapter Madame Bonacieux will be accompanied by someone d'Artagnan again believes is her lover, but then we find out that it is Lord Buckingham, the queen's lover . . . Why not think that the mix-up over the streets is intentional—that it functions as a sign and allegory of the mix-up over people and that there are subtle parallels between the two kinds of misunderstanding?

The answer is that, throughout the novel, cases of mistaken identity are followed by sudden recognitions, as is usual in nine-teenth-century popular novels. D'Artagnan continually recognizes in a passing stranger the infamous man of Meung; many times he believes that Madame Bonacieux is unfaithful and then discovers that she is as pure as an angel. Athos will recognize Milady as Anne de Breuil, whom he married years before discovering she was a criminal. Milady will recognize in the executioner of Lille the brother of the man she drove to ruin. And so forth. The anachronism concerning the rue Servandoni, however, is not followed by any revelation, and Aramis keeps living in that nowhere until the end of the novel and probably afterward. According to the rules of nineteenth-century cloak-and-dagger novels, if we follow the Servandoni trail we find ourselves in a blind alley.

Up to now we've been conducting some amusing mental experiments, asking ourselves what would have happened if Nerval had told us that the carriage hadn't been pulled by a horse, if Rex Stout had situated Alexanderplatz in New York, if Dumas had made d'Artagnan turn onto the rue Bonaparte. All right, so we've enjoyed ourselves, as philosophers do sometimes; but we must not forget that Nerval never said the carriage lacked a horse, that Stout never did put Alexanderplatz in New York, and that d'Artagnan never turned onto the rue Bonaparte.

The encyclopedic competence demanded of the reader (the limits placed on the potentially infinite size of the maximal Encyclopedia, which none of us will ever possess) is limited by the fictional text. Probably a model reader of Dumas should know that Bonaparte couldn't have had a road named after him in 1625, and in fact Dumas doesn't make that mistake. Probably that same reader is not supposed to know who Servandoni was, and Dumas can permit himself to mention him in the wrong place. A fictional text suggests some capacities that the reader should have, and sets up others. Regarding the rest, the text remains vague, but of course it doesn't oblige us to explore the entire maximal Encyclopedia.

The precise format of the Encyclopedia that a text requires a reader to have remains a matter of conjecture. To discover it means discovering the strategy of the model author—that is, not the figure in the carpet but the *rule* by which many figures can be traced in the fictional carpet.

What is the moral of this story? It is that fictional texts come to the aid of our metaphysical narrowmindedness. We live in the great labyrinth of the actual world, which is bigger and more complex than the world of Little Red Riding Hood. It is a world whose paths we have not yet entirely mapped out and whose total structure we are unable to describe. In the hope that rules of the game exist, humanity throughout the centuries has speculated about whether this labyrinth has an author, or perhaps more than one. And it has thought of God, or the gods, as if they were empirical authors, narrators, or model authors. People have wondered what an empirical divinity might be like: whether it has a beard, whether it's a He, a She, or an IT, whether it was born or has always existed, and even (in our own times) whether it's dead. God as Narrator has always been sought—in the intestines of animals, in the flittings of birds, in the burning bush, in the first sentence of the Ten Commandments. But some (including philosophers, of course, but also adherents of many religions) have searched for God as Model Author—that is, God as the Rule of the Game, as the Law that makes or someday will make the labyrinth of the world understandable. The Divinity in this case is something we must discover at the same time we discover why we are in the labyrinth, and what path we are being asked to walk within it.

In my postscript to *The Name of the Rose,* I said that we like detective stories because they ask the same question as the one posed by philosophy and religion: "Whodunnit?"[9] But this is metaphysics for a first-level reader. The second-level reader makes greater demands: How must I identify (conjecturally) or even how must I construct the Model Author so that my reading makes sense? Stephen Dedalus wondered: If a man hacking randomly at a block of wood makes the image of a cow, is that image a work of art? And if it isn't, why not?[10] Today, since we have formulated a poetics of the *ready-made,* we know the answer: that casual form is a work of art if we manage to imagine the shaping strategy of an author behind it. This is an extreme case, in which becoming a good reader necessarily entails becoming a good author. But it is an extreme case that expresses wonderfully well the indissoluble bond, the dialectic, between author and model reader.

In this dialectic, we must follow the precept of the oracle of Delphi: Know Thyself. And since, as Heraclitus reminds us, "the Lord whose oracle is at Delphi neither speaks nor conceals, but indicates through signs," the knowledge we seek is unlimited because it assumes the form of a continuous interrogation.

Such an interrogation, although potentially infinite, is limited by the abridged format of the Encyclopedia requested by a work of fiction, whereas we are not sure whether the actual world, along with the infinity of its possible doubles, is infinite and limited or finite and unlimited. But there is another reason fiction makes us feel more metaphysically comfortable than reality. There is a golden rule that cryptanalysts and code breakers rely on—namely, that every secret message can be deciphered, provided one knows that it is a message. The problem with the actual world is that, since the dawn of time, humans have been wondering whether there is a message and, if so, whether this message makes sense. With fictional universes, we know without a doubt that they do have a message and that an authorial entity stands behind them as creator, as well as within them as a set of reading instructions.

Thus, our quest for the model author is an Ersatz for that other quest, in the course of which the Image of the Father fades into the Fog of the Infinity, and we never stop wondering why there is something rather than nothing.

FICTIONAL PROTOCOLS	If fictional worlds are so comfortable, why not try to read the actual world as if it were a work of fiction? Or, if fictional worlds are so small and deceptively comfortable, why not try to de-

vise fictional worlds that are as complex, contradictory, and provocative as the actual one?

Let me answer the second question first: Dante, Rabelais, Shakespeare, Joyce indeed did this. And Nerval. In my writings on "open works," I am referring precisely to works of literature that strive to be as ambiguous as life. It is true that in *Sylvie* we know without a doubt that Adrienne died in 1832 (whereas we are not equally sure that Napoleon died in 1821—since he could have been secretly rescued from Saint Helena by Julien Sorel, leaving a double there in his place, and may subsequently have lived under the name of Père Dodu in Loisy, where he encountered the narrator in 1830). The rest of Sylvie's story, however—all that ambiguous interplay between life and dream, past and present—is more similar to the uncertainty that prevails in our everyday life than it is to the adamant certainty with which we, and Scarlett O'Hara, know that tomorrow is another day.

Let me now answer the first question. In my book *The Open Work,* I commented on the strategy of live TV broadcasts, which try to frame the fortuitous flow of events by giving it a narrative structure; I noted that life is certainly more like *Ulysses* than like *The Three Musketeers*—yet we are all more inclined to think of it in terms of *The Three Musketeers* than in terms of *Ulysses.*[1] My character Jacopo Belbo, in *Foucault's Pendulum,* seems to praise such a natural inclination when he says:

> No true dandy, I thought, would have made love to Scarlett O'Hara or even to Constance Bonacieux . . . I played with the dime novel, in order to take a stroll outside of life . . . But I was wrong . . . Proust was right: life is represented better by bad music than by a Missa Solemnis. Great Art . . . shows us the art as the artists would like the world to be. The dime novel, however, pretends to joke, but then it shows the world as it actually is—or at least the world as it will become. Women are a lot more like Milady than they are like Little Nell, Fu Manchu is more real than Nathan the Wise, and History is closer to what Sue narrates than to what Hegel projects.[2]

A bitter remark indeed, by a disenchanted character. But it portrays our natural tendency to interpret what happens to us in terms of what Barthes called a *"texte lisible,"* a *readerly text.* Since fiction seems a more comfortable environment than life, we try to read life as if it were a piece of fiction.

In my final lecture here, I'll be dealing with various cases in which we are compelled to transpose fiction and life—to read life as if it were fiction, to read fiction as if it were life. Some of these confusions are pleasant and innocent, some absolutely necessary, some frightening.

In 1934 Carlo Emilio Gadda published a newspaper article which described the slaughterhouse in Milan. Since Gadda was a great writer, that article was also a fine specimen of prose. Andrea Bonomi has recently suggested an interesting experiment.[3] Let's imagine that the article never mentioned the city of Milan but simply spoke of "this city," that it remained in typewritten form among Gadda's unpublished papers, and that today a researcher finds it but is not sure whether it describes a fragment of the real world or is a piece of fiction. And so she does not ask herself whether or not the statements the text contains are true; rather, she enjoys reconstructing a universe, the universe of the slaughterhouse of an unidentified—and perhaps imaginary—city. Later the researcher discovers another copy of the article in the archives of the Milan slaughterhouse; on this copy the director of the slaughterhouse many years ago inserted a marginal remark which says, "Note: this is a totally accurate description." Thus, Gadda's text is an allegedly faithful report about a precise place existing in the actual world. Bonomi's point is that although the researcher must change her views on the nature of the text, she does not need to reread it. The world it describes, the inhabitants of that world, and all the properties of both are the same; the researcher will simply map that representation onto reality. As Bonomi puts it, "In order for us to grasp the content of an account describing a certain state of affairs, we do not need to apply the categories of true or false to that content."

This is not such a commonsensical statement. As a matter of fact, we tend to think that usually when we listen to or read any kind of verbal account, we assume that the speaker or the writer intends to tell us something we are supposed to take as true, and so we are prepared to evaluate his or her statement in terms of truth or falsity. Likewise we commonly think that only in exceptional cases—those in which a fictional signal appears—do we suspend disbelief and prepare to enter an imaginary world. The thought-experiment with Gadda's text proves, on the contrary, that when listening to a series of statements recounting what happened to someone in such-and-such a place, we initially cooperate in reconstructing a universe possessing a kind of internal cohesion—and only later do we decide whether we should take those statements as a description of the actual world or of an imaginary one.

This calls into question a distinction which has been proposed by many theorists—namely, that between *natural* and *artificial* narrative.[4] Natural narrative describes events that actually occurred (or which the speaker mendaciously or mistakenly claims actually occurred). Examples of natural narrative are my account of what happened to me yesterday, a newspaper report, or even Gibbon's *History of the Decline and Fall of the Roman Empire.* Artificial narrative is supposedly represented by fiction, which only *pretends* to tell the truth about the actual universe, or which claims to tell the truth about a fictional universe.

We usually recognize artificial narrative thanks to the "paratext"—that is, the external messages that surround a text. A typical paratextual signal for fictional narrative is the designation "A Novel" on the book's cover. Sometimes even the author's name can function in this way; thus, nineteenth-century readers knew that a book whose title page announced it was "by the author of Waverly" was unmistakably a piece of fiction. The most obvious textual (that is, internal) signal of fictionality is an introductory formula such as "Once upon a time."

Yet things are not as clear cut as they may seem from a theoretical point of view. Take, for example, the historic incident caused in 1938 by Orson Welles's false radio broadcast about an invasion from Mars. Misunderstanding and even panic resulted from the fact that some listeners believed all radio news broadcasts are examples of natural narrative, whereas Welles thought he had provided listeners with a sufficient number of fictional signals. But many listeners tuned in after the broadcast had already begun; others did not understand the fictional signals and proceeded to map the content of the broadcast onto the actual world.

My friend Giorgio Celli, who is a writer and a professor of entomology, once wrote a short story about the perfect crime. Both he and I were characters in this story. Celli (the fictional character) injected a tube of toothpaste with a chemical substance that sexually attracts wasps. Eco (the fictional character) brushed his teeth with this toothpaste before going to bed, and a small amount of it remained on his lips. Swarms of sexually aroused wasps were thus attracted to his face, and their stings were fatal to poor Eco. The story was published on the third page of the Bologna newspaper *Il resto del carlino*. As you may or may not know, Italian newspapers, at least until several years ago, generally devoted page three to arts and letters. The article called the "elzeviro" in the left-hand column of the page could be a review, a short essay, or even a short story. Celli's short story appeared as a literary feature entitled "How I Murdered Umberto Eco." The editors evidently had confidence in their basic assumption: readers know that everything printed in a newspaper must be taken seriously except for items on the literary page, which must or can be considered examples of artificial narrative.

But that morning, when I walked into the café near my house, I was greeted by the waiters with expressions of joy and relief, for they thought Celli had actually murdered me. I attributed this incident to the fact that their cultural background did not equip them to recognize journalistic conventions. Later in the day, however, I happened to see the dean of my college, a highly educated man who of course knows all there is to know about the difference between text and paratext, natural and artificial narrative, and so on. He told me that, on reading the paper that morning, he had been taken aback. Though the shock had not lasted long, the appearance of that title in a newspaper—a textual framework where by definition true events are recounted—had momentarily misled him.

It has been said that artificial narrative is recognizable because it is more complex than the natural kind. But any attempt to determine the structural differences between natural and artificial narrative can usually be falsified by a series of counterexamples. We might, for instance, define fiction as narrative in which characters perform certain actions or undergo certain experiences, and in which these actions and passions transform a character's situation from an initial state to a final one. Yet this definition could also apply to a story that is both serious and truthful, such as: "Last night I was famished. I went out to eat. I had steak and lobster, and after that I felt content."

If we add that these actions must be difficult and must entail dramatic and unexpected choices, I am sure that W. C. Fields would have known how to fashion a dramatic account of how he was overcome with anguish at the prospect of having to make the difficult choice between steak and lobster, and how he succeeded in solving his predicament brilliantly. Nor can we say that the choices confronting the characters in *Ulysses* are any more dramatic than the ones we must make in our daily lives. Not even Aristotelian precepts (according to which the hero of a story must be neither better nor worse than us, must experience unexpected recognitions, and must be subjected to rapid turns of fortune until the point at which the action reaches a catastrophic climax, followed by catharsis) are enough to define a work of fiction: many of Plutarch's *Lives* also meet these requirements.

Fictionality seems to be revealed by an insistence on unverifiable details and introspective intrusions, since no historical report can support such "reality effects." Roland Barthes, however, has cited a passage from Michelet's *Histoire de France* (volume 5, *La Révolution,* 1869) in which the author employs this fictional device when describing Charlotte Corday's imprisonment: "Au bout d'une heure et demie, on frappa doucement à une petite porte qui était derrière elle" ("After an hour and a half, somebody knocked softly at the little door behind her").[5]

As for explicit introductory fictional signals, one would of course never find them at the beginning of any natural narratives. Thus, despite its title, *A True Story* by Lucianus of Samosata must be considered fictional, since in the second paragraph the author clearly states, "I have presented lies of all kinds under the guise of truth and reliability." Similarly, Fielding begins *Tom Jones* by warning the reader that he is introducing a novel. But another typical indication of fictionality is the false assertion of truthfulness at the outset of a story. Compare these examples of incipits:

> I was prompted by the just and insistent requests of the most
> learned brothers . . . to ask myself why there is no one today

who could write a chronicle, in any literary form, so that we might hand down to our descendants an account of the many events that have taken place both in God's churches and among peoples, events that deserve to be known.

Never have grandeur and gallantry shone so brightly in France as during the last years under the reign of Henry II.

The first is the beginning of the *Historia suorum temporum,* by Rudolph Glaber; the second is from *La Princesse de Clèves,* by Madame de Lafayette. It should be pointed out that the latter passage goes on for pages and pages before revealing to the reader that it is the opening of a novel and not of a chronicle.

On August 16, 1968, I was handed a book written by a certain Abbé Vallet . . . Supplemented by historical information that was actually quite scant, the book claimed to reproduce faithfully a fourteenth-century manuscript.

When Caesar saw certain rich strangers holding puppies and baby monkeys in their arms, caressing them, he asked (it is said) whether their women bore children.

The second incipit, which seems to be fiction, is the beginning of Plutarch's "Life of Pericles," whereas the first is the beginning of my novel *The Name of the Rose.*

If ever the story of any private man's adventures in the world were worth making public, and were acceptable when published, the Editor of this account thinks this will be so. The wonders of this man's life exceed all that (he thinks) is to be found extant . . . The Editor believes the thing to be a just history of fact; neither is there any appearance of fiction in it.

It may not be unacceptable to our readers that we should take this opportunity of presenting them with a slight sketch of the greatest king that has, in modern times, succeeded by right of birth to a throne. It may, we fear, be impossible to compress so long and eventful a story within the limits which we must prescribe to ourselves.

The first excerpt is the beginning of *Robinson Crusoe;* the second is the beginning of Macaulay's essay on Frederick the Great.

> I must not begin to narrate the events of my life without first mentioning my good parents, whose characters and lovingness were to so greatly influence my education and my well-being.

> It is a little remarkable, that—though disinclined to talk over-much of myself and my affairs at the fireside, and to my personal friends—an autobiographical impulse should twice in my life have taken possession of me, in addressing the public.

The first passage is the beginning of the memoirs of Giuseppe Garibaldi; the second is from *The Scarlet Letter,* by Nathaniel Hawthorne.

Fairly explicit fictional signals do exist, of course—for instance, the *in medias res* beginning, an opening dialogue, insistence on an individual story rather than on a general one, and, above all, immediate signals of irony, as in Robert Musil's novel *The Man without Qualities,* which starts with a lengthy description of the weather, full of technical terms:

> There was a depression over the Atlantic. It was traveling eastward, toward an area of high pressure over Russia, and still showed no tendency to move northward around it. The isotherms and isotheres were fulfilling their function. The atmospheric temperature was in proper relation to the average annual temperature.

Musil goes on for half a page and then remarks:

> In short, to use an expression that describes the facts pretty satisfactorily, even though it is somewhat old-fashioned: it was a fine August day in the year 1913.

It is enough, however, to find just one work of fiction that does not display any of these features (we could provide dozens of examples) to argue that an incontrovertible signal of fictionality does not exist. But, as we noted earlier, elements of paratext can supervene.

In such a case, what very often occurs is that one does not decide to enter a fictional world; one happens to find oneself within that world. After a while, one becomes aware of this and decides that what is happening is a dream. As Novalis said, "You are about to awake when you dream that you are dreaming." But this state of half sleep—a state in which the narrator of *Sylvie* finds himself—poses many problems.

In fiction, precise references to the actual world are so closely linked that, after spending some time in the world of the novel and mixing fictional elements with references to reality, as one should, the reader no longer knows exactly where he or she stands. Such a state gives rise to some well-known phenomena. The most common is when the reader maps the fictional model onto reality—in other words, when the reader comes to believe in the actual existence of fictional characters and events. The fact that many people believed and still believe that Sherlock Holmes really existed is only the most famous of a great many possible examples. If you have ever visited Dublin with some Joyce fans, you will know that after a while it is extremely difficult, both for them and for you, to separate the city described by Joyce from the real one; and the conflation has become even easier now that scholars have identified the individuals Joyce used as models. As you walk along the canals or climb the Martello Tower, you begin to confuse Gogarthy with Lynch or Cranly and young Joyce with Stephen Dedalus.

In speaking of Nerval, Proust says that "a shiver runs down one's spine when one reads the name 'Pontarmé' in a railway guide."[6] Having realized that *Sylvie* is about a man who dreams of a dream, Proust dreams about Valois, which actually exists, in the absurd hope of once again finding the girl who has become part of his own dreams.

Taking fictional characters seriously can also produce an unusual type of intertextuality: a character from a particular fictional work may appear in another fictional work and thus act as a signal of truthfulness. This is what happens in Rostand's *Cyrano de Bergerac* at the end of Act 2, where the hero is congratulated by a musketeer, admiringly introduced as "d'Artagnan." The presence of d'Artagnan is a guarantee of the truthfulness of Cyrano's story—even though d'Artagnan was a minor historical figure (known mainly through Dumas), whereas Cyrano was a famous writer.

When fictional characters begin migrating from text to text, they have acquired citizenship in the real world and have freed themselves from the story that created them.

I once came up with the following idea for a novel (since postmodern narrative has by now inured readers to every possible metafictional depravity):

Vienna, 1950. Twenty years have gone by, but Sam Spade has not given up his search for the Maltese falcon. His contact now is Harry Lime, and they are talking furtively at the top of the Prater's Ferris wheel. They come down and walk over to the Mozart Café, where Sam is playing "As Time Goes By" on the lyre. At a table in the back, a cigarette hanging from the corner of his mouth, a bitter expression on his face, sits Rick. He has found a clue in the papers Ugarte has shown him, and now he shows Sam Spade a photograph of Ugarte: "Cairo!" murmurs the detective. Rick goes on with his account: when he triumphantly entered Paris with Captain Renault, as a member of De Gaulle's liberating army, he heard about a certain Dragon Lady (allegedly the assassin of Robert Jordan during the Spanish Civil War), whom the secret service had put on the trail of the falcon. She should be here any minute. The door opens and a woman appears. "Ilsa!" Rick cries. "Brigid!" Sam Spade cries. "Anna Schmidt!" Lime cries. "Miss Scarlett!" Sam cries, "you're back! Don't make my boss suffer any more."

Out of the darkness of the bar comes a man with a sarcastic smile on his face. It's Philip Marlowe. "Let's go, Miss Marple," he says to the woman. "Father Brown is waiting for us on Baker Street."

When does it become easy to attribute a real life to a fictional character? This is not the fate of all fictional characters. It did not happen to Gargantua, to Don Quixote, to Madame Bovary, to Long John Silver, to Lord Jim, or to Popeye (either Faulkner's Popeye or the comic book one). Instead, it happened to Sherlock Holmes, Siddhartha, Leopold Bloom, and Rick Blaine. I believe that the extratextual and intratextual life of characters coincides with cult phenomena. Why does a movie become a cult movie? Why does a novel or a poem become a cult book?

Some time ago, while trying to explain why *Casablanca* has become a cult movie, I proposed the hypothesis that one factor contributing to the development of a cult around a particular work is the "disjointedness" of the work. But disjointedness also entails the possibility of being "put out of joint"—a notion that needs some explaining. It is now common knowledge that *Casablanca* was shot day by day without anyone knowing how the story would end. Ingrid Bergman looks charmingly mysterious in the film because, while acting her role, she did not know which man she would choose, and so gave both of them her tender and ambiguous smile. We also know that, in order to advance the plot, the scriptwriters put all the clichés of cinematic and narrative history into the film, turning it into a museum, so to speak, for moviegoers. For this reason, it can be used as a kit for assembling archetypes. In a way, the same thing applies to *The Rocky Horror Picture Show*, which is the cult movie par excellence precisely because it lacks form, and so can be endlessly deformed and put out of joint. We should note also, however, that T. S. Eliot, in a famous essay, ventured the view that this was the reason for the success of *Hamlet*.

According to Eliot, *Hamlet* resulted from the blending of three different source works in which the motive was revenge, in which delays were caused by the difficulty in assassinating a king surrounded by guards, and in which madness was Hamlet's deliberate and effective means of escaping suspicion. Shakespeare, in contrast, dealt with the effect of a mother's guilt upon her son, and was unable to impose his motive successfully upon the "intractable" material of his sources. Thus, "the delay in revenge is unexplained on grounds of necessity or expediency; and the effect of the 'madness' is not to lull but to arouse the king's suspicion . . . And probably more people have thought Hamlet a work of art because they found it interesting, than have found it interesting because it is a work of art. It is the Mona Lisa of literature."[7]

The immense and age-old popularity of the Bible is due to its disjointed nature, stemming from the fact that it was written by several different authors. The *Divine Comedy* is not disjointed at all, but because of its complexity, the number of characters it deals with, and the events it recounts (everything concerning heaven and earth, as Dante said), every line of it can be put out of joint and used as a magic spell or as a mnemonic device. Some fanatics have even gone so far as to take it as a basis for trivia games, just as Virgil's *Aeneid* was used in the Middle Ages as a manual for prophecies and divination, like Nostradamus' *Centuries* (another excellent example of success due to radical, irremediable disjointedness). But although the *Divine Comedy* can be put out of joint, the *Decameron* cannot, since each tale is to be taken in its entirety. The extent to which a particular work can be put out of joint does not depend on its aesthetic value. *Hamlet* is still a fascinating work (and not even Eliot can persuade us to love it less), whereas I do not believe that even *Rocky Horror* addicts would feel inclined to credit it with Shakespearean greatness. Yet both *Hamlet* and *Rocky Horror* are cult objects, since the former is "disjointable," while the latter is so disjointed as to allow all kinds of interactive games. In order to become a Sacred Wood, a wood must be tangled and twisted like the forests of the Druids, and not orderly like a French garden.

There are, then, many reasons a work of fiction may be

mapped onto real life. But we must also consider another, far more important problem: our tendency to construct life as a novel.

According to the Judeo-Christian myth of origins, Adam named all creatures and things. In the age-old search for the perfect language (which will be the topic of my next book), attempts have been made to reconstruct the language of Adam, who is said to have known how to name things and creatures according to their nature. For centuries it was believed that Adam had invented a nomenclature—that is, a list of rigid designators—consisting of names of "natural kinds," so that he could give a "true" label to horses, apples, or oak trees. During the seventeenth century Francis Lodwick put forward the idea that original names were the names not of substances but of actions; in other words, there was no original name for the drinker or the drink, but there was such a name for the act of drinking. It was from the sphere of action, Lodwick claimed, that the names of the doer (the drinker), the object (the drink), and the place (the drinking house) derived. Lodwick's notions preceded what today is called the theory of *case grammar* (of which Kenneth Burke was an early proponent), according to which our understanding of a given term in a given context takes the form of an instruction: "There should be an agent, a counteragent, a goal, and so on." In short, we understand sentences because we are able to imagine short stories, to which these sentences refer even when they are naming a given natural kind.

We can find a similar idea in Plato's "Cratylus": a word represents not a thing in itself but the source or the result of an action. The genitive form for Jupiter is *Dios* because such an original name expressed the usual activity of the king of gods—that is, to be *di' on zen,* "the one through whom life is given." Likewise *anthropos* ("man") is seen as the corruption of an earlier syntagma meaning "the one who is able to reconsider what has seen."

Thus, we could say that Adam did not distinguish tigers (for example) merely as individual specimens of a natural kind. He distinguished particular animals, endowed with certain morphological properties, insofar as they were involved in certain types of action, interacting with other animals and with their natural environment. Then he stated that the subject (usually acting against certain countersubjects in order to achieve certain goals, and usually showing up in specific circumstances) was only part of a story—the story being inseparable from the subject, and the subject being an indispensable part of the story. Only at this stage of world-knowledge could the subject *X-in-action* be labeled "tiger."

Today, in the field of artificial intelligence, specialists use the word "frames" to mean action schemes (such as entering a restaurant, going to the station to catch a train, opening an umbrella). Once a computer has learned these schemes, it is able to understand different situations. But psychologists such as Jerome Bruner argue that our normal way of accounting for everyday experiences likewise takes the form of stories,[8] and the same thing occurs with History seen as *historia rerum gestarum,* or narration of past real events. Arthur Danto said that "history tells stories," and Hayden White spoke of "history as a literary artifact."[9] A. J. Greimas has founded the whole of his semiotic theory upon an "actantial model," a sort of narrative skeleton which represents the deepest structure of every semiosic process, so that "narrativity is . . . the organizing principle of *all* discourse."[10]

Our perceptual relationship with the world works because we trust prior stories. We could not fully perceive a tree if we did not know (because others have told us) that it is the product of a long growth process and that it does not grow overnight. This certainty is part of our "understanding" that a tree is a tree, and not a flower. We accept a story that our ancestors have handed down to us as being true, even though today we call these ancestors scientists.

No one lives in the immediate present; we link things and events thanks to the adhesive function of memory, both personal and collective (history and myth). We rely upon a previous tale when, in saying "I," we do not question that we are the natural continuation of an individual who (according to our parents or the registry office) was born at that precise time, on that precise day, in that precise year, and in that precise place. Living with two memories (our individual memory, which enables us to relate what we did yesterday, and the collective memory, which tells us when and where our mother was born), we often tend to confuse them, as if we had witnessed the birth of our mother (and also Julius Caesar's) in the same way we "witnessed" the scenes of our own past experiences.

This tangle of individual and collective memory prolongs our life, by extending it back through time, and appears to us as a promise of immortality. When we partake of this collective memory (through the tales of our elders or through books), we are like Borges gazing at the magical Aleph—the point that contains the entire universe: in the course of our lifetime we can, in a way, shiver along with Napoleon as a sudden gust of cold wind sweeps over Saint Helena, rejoice with Henry V over the victory at Agincourt, and suffer with Caesar as a result of Brutus' betrayal.

And so it is easy to understand why fiction fascinates us so. It offers us the opportunity to employ limitlessly our faculties for perceiving the world and reconstructing the past. Fiction has the same function that games have. In playing, children learn to live, because they simulate situations in which they may find themselves as adults. And it is through fiction that we adults train our ability to structure our past and present experience.

But if narrative activity is so closely linked to our everyday life, couldn't it be that we interpret life as fiction, and that in interpreting reality we introduce fictional elements?

I would like to cite a disconcerting story which was always clearly fictional—because it was founded on explicit quotations from fictional sources—yet which many people have unfortunately taken to be true history.

The construction of our story began a long time ago, at the beginning of the fourteenth century, when Philip the Fair destroyed the Knights Templars. Since then, numerous tales have been invented concerning the clandestine activities of the survivors of the order. Even today we can find dozens of recent works on this subject, on the bookshelves usually labeled "New Age."

In the seventeenth century, another story originated—that of the Rosy Cross. The Brotherhood of the Rosy Cross first appeared on the scene in the descriptions contained in the Manifestos of the Rosy Cross (*Fama fraternitatis*, 1614; *Confessio roseae crucis*, 1615). The author or authors of the Manifestos are unknown, officially, because those to whom authorship was attributed denied it. The Manifestos gave rise to a series of activities on the part of those who believed in the existence of the brotherhood, and who were thereby expressing their ardent desire to become members themselves. Aside from a few hints, no one admitted to belonging to the brotherhood, because the group was secret and Rosicrucian writers typically claimed that they were not Rosicrucians. This implies that, ipso facto, all those who later claimed to be Rosicrucians were certainly not. As a consequence, not only is there no historical proof of the existence of Rosicrucians, but by definition there can be none. In the seventeenth century Heinrich Neuhaus was able to "demonstrate" that they existed, supporting his claim with this extraordinary argument: "Simply because they change their names and lie about their age, and because through their own admission they come and go without being recognized, no logical person can deny that they must necessarily exist" (*Pia et ultimissima admonestatio de fratribus Roseae Crucis*, Danzig, 1618). In the centuries that have passed since then, adherents have formed countless esoteric groups that have claimed to be the sole and true heirs of the original Rosicrucians and to possess indisputable documents—which, however, cannot be shown to anyone, as they are secret.

In the eighteenth century a French branch of Freemasonry called Scottish Freemasonry (also known as Templar and Occultist Freemasonry) became part of this fictional construction. Not only did Scottish Freemasons trace their origins to the builders of Solomon's Temple, but they also claimed that the builders of the Temple were related to the Templars, whose secret tradition supposedly had been handed down through the mediation of the Rosicrucians. These secret societies and the possible existence of "Unknown Superiors" guiding the fate of the world were the subject of debate in the days just prior to the French Revolution. In 1789 the Marquis de Luchet warned that "in the bosom of the deepest darkness a society has been formed, a society of new beings, who know one another although they have never seen one another . . . From the Jesuits' system of rule, this society adopts blind obedience; from the Masons, it takes its trials and ceremonies; and from the Templars, its subterranean mysteries and its great audacity" (*Essai sur la secte des illuminés,* 1789).

Between 1797 and 1798, in an effort to account for the French Revolution, Abbé Barruel wrote his *Mémoires pour servir à l'histoire du jacobinisme,* a supposedly factual book that reads like a dime novel. It begins, naturally, with a discussion of the Templars. After the burning of their Great Master Molay, they allegedly transformed themselves into a secret society dedicated to destroying the papacy and all monarchies and to creating a world republic. In the eighteenth century they took over Freemasonry and created a sort of academy (whose evil members were Voltaire, Turgot, Condorcet, Diderot, and d'Alembert); they were also responsible for the founding of the Jacobins. But the Jacobins were controlled by an even more secret society, that of the Illuminati of Bavaria—regicides by vocation. Thus, the French Revolution, according to Barruel, was the final result of an age-old plot.

Even Napoleon requested reports about clandestine sects. The author of these reports was Charles de Berkheim, who—as spies and informers usually do—got his information from public sources and gave Napoleon, as a fantastic scoop, all the news that Napoleon himself could have read in the books of the Marquis de Luchet and Barruel. Apparently, Napoleon was so impressed by these horrifying descriptions of a directorate of Unknown Superiors capable of ruling the world, that he did his best to join the group.

Barruel's *Mémoires* did not contain any reference to the Jews. But in 1806 he received a letter from a certain Captain Simonini, who claimed that Mani (the founder of Manichaeism) and the Old Man of the Mountain (grand master of the secret order of Assassins and allegedly a notorious ally of the early Templars) were Jews, that Masonry had been founded by the Jews, and that the Jews had infiltrated all the existing secret societies. It seems that Simonini's letter had in fact been concocted by the agents of minister of police Joseph Fouché, who was worried that Napoleon, for political reasons, was getting in touch with the French Jewish community.

Barruel was frightened by Simonini's revelations and is alleged to have said in private that publication of the letter could cause a massacre of the Jews. Nevertheless, he composed an essay in which he accepted Simonini's ideas, and, although he destroyed this text, rumors had already begun to spread. They did not produce interesting results until the middle of the century, when the Jesuits became alarmed by the anticlerical fathers of the Italian Risorgimento, such as Garibaldi, who were affiliated with Masonry. They adopted, as polemically useful, the claim that Italian carbonari were the agents of a Judeo-Masonic plot.

But in the nineteenth century, anticlericals were likewise trying to defame the Jesuits by showing that they were plotting against mankind. This is true of many "serious" writers (from Michelet and Quinet to Garibaldi and Gioberti); but it was a novelist, Eugène Sue, who gave the greatest publicity to such allegations. In Sue's novel *The Wandering Jew,* the evil Monsieur Rodin, the incarnation of the Jesuit world conspiracy, is clearly another romanesque version of the Unknown Superiors. Monsieur Rodin returns in Sue's last novel, *The Mysteries of the People,* where the Jesuits' diabolical plan is exposed down to the last criminal detail in a document sent to Rodin (fictional character) by the head of the order, Father Roothaan (historical figure). Sue also brings in another fictional character, Rodolphe of Gerolstein, from his novel *The Mysteries of Paris* (a real cult book, to such an extent that thousands of readers were sending letters to its characters). Gerolstein comes into possession of this document and reveals "how cunningly this infernal plot is ordered, and what frightful sorrows, what horrendous enslavement, what terrible despotism it would spell for Europe and the world, were it to succeed."

In 1864, after Sue's novels had appeared, a certain Maurice Joly wrote a liberal pamphlet criticizing Napoleon III in which Machiavelli, who represents the dictator's cynicism, talks with Montesquieu. The Jesuit plot elaborated by Sue (along with the same classical formula, "the end justifies the means") is now attributed to Napoleon—and I have detected in this pamphlet no less than seven pages that are, if not plagiarized, at least laden with generous and unconfessed quotations from Sue. Joly was arrested for his anti-imperial writings, served fifteen months in prison, and then committed suicide. Exit Joly, but we shall encounter him again further on.

In 1868 Hermann Goedsche, a German postal employee who had previously published false and libelous political tracts, wrote, under the pen name Sir John Retcliffe, a popular novel titled *Biarritz* in which he described an occultist scene in the cemetery of Prague. Goedsche modeled this scene on the meeting (described in 1849 by Dumas in *Joseph Balsamo*) between Cagliostro, chief of the Unknown Superiors, and a group of other Illuminati, who plotted the Affair of the Diamond Necklace. But instead of depicting Cagliostro & Company, Goedsche restaged the scene using representatives of the twelve tribes of Israel, who gather to prepare the Jewish conquest of the world, which is foretold in detail by their great rabbi. Five years later the same story was reused in a Russian pamphlet ("The Jews, Masters of the World") but as if it were a serious report. In 1881 the French periodical *Le Contemporain* republished the same story, claiming that it had come from an unimpeachable source, the English diplomat Sir John Readcliff. In 1896 François Bournand again quoted the discourses of the great rabbi (whom he called John Readclif) in his book *Les Juifs, nos contemporains*. From this point on, the fictive meeting invented by Dumas, embellished with the projects invented by Sue, and attributed by Joly to Napoleon III became the "real" discourse of the great rabbi and reappeared in several other places.

The story does not stop here. At the turn of the twentieth century, Peter Ivanovich Rachkovsky (not a fictional character, but worthy of being one), a Russian who had once been arrested for his involvement with leftist revolutionary groups and who had later become a police informer, joined the ranks of the extreme right-wing terrorist organization known as the Black Hundreds and was ultimately appointed chief of the Okhrana, the czar's political police. In order to help his political sponsor, Count Sergei Witte, against one of his political opponents, Elie de Cyon, Rachkovsky carried out a search of Cyon's home; there he found a pamphlet in which Cyon had copied Joly's pamphlet excoriating Napoleon III—having "corrected" it, however, so as to attribute the same ideas to Witte. Since Rachkovsky, like any follower of the Black Hundreds, was a ferocious anti-Semite (and these events occurred about the time of the Dreyfus affair), he created a new romanesque version of that old text, deleting all the references to Witte and attributing the plot to the Jews. The name "Cyon" evoked "Zion," and Rachkovsky figured that a Jewish plot denounced by a Jew could become highly credible.

The text created by Rachkovsky was probably the first source of the *Protocols of the Learned Elders of Zion*. The *Protocols* are clearly fictional, since in them the Elders brazenly spell out their evil projects; and though this might be believable in a novel by Sue, it exceeds the bounds of credibility that anyone would do this so shamelessly in reality. The Elders candidly declare, "We have unlimited ambition, an all-consuming greed, a merciless desire for revenge, and an intense hatred." But—as in the case of Hamlet, according to Eliot—the variety of narrative sources makes this text rather incongruous.

In the *Protocols*, the Elders want to abolish freedom of the press but encourage libertinage. They criticize liberalism but support the idea of multinational corporations. They advocate revolution in every country, but in order to arouse the masses they want to exacerbate inequality. They plan to build underground railways, so as to have a way of mining the big cities. They claim that the end justifies the means and are in favor of anti-Semitism, both to control the numbers of Jewish poor and to soften the hearts of Gentiles in the face of Jewish tragedy. They call for abolishing the study of the classics and of ancient history and want to institute sports and visual education (that is, education through images) to stultify the working class. And so on.

As scholars have noted, it is easy to see that the *Protocols* were a product of nineteenth-century France, since they are full of references to fin-de-siècle French issues (such as the Panama scandal, and the rumors about the presence of Jewish shareholders in the Paris Métro Company). It is also clear that they were based on a lot of well-known novels. Alas, the story, once again, was so narratively convincing that many people had no trouble taking it seriously. The rest is History: in Russia, an itinerant monk named Sergei Nilus—a bizarre figure, half prophet and half scoundrel, who had long been obsessed with the idea of the Antichrist—in order to further his ambition of becoming spiritual adviser to the czar, prefaced and published the text of the *Protocols*. Subsequently, this text traveled around Europe until it fell into the hands of Hitler. You know the rest of the story.[11]

Nobody realized that such an incredible concoction of sources (see Figure 14) was a work of fiction? Of course, some people did. In 1921, at least, the *Times* of London discovered the old pamphlet by Joly and realized that it was the source of the *Protocols*. But evidence is not enough for those who want to live in a horror novel. In 1924 Nesta Webster, who devoted her life to

Figure 14

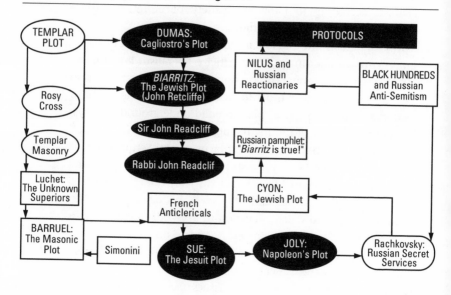

supporting the story of the Unknown Superiors and the Jewish plot, wrote a book entitled *Secret Societies and Subversive Movements*. She was thoroughly informed, was aware of the *Times*'s revelations, and knew the entire history of Nilus, Rachkovsky, Goedsche, and so on. (She was ignorant only of the connections with Dumas and Sue, which are my own discovery.) Here is her conclusion: "The only opinion to which I have committed myself is that, whether genuine or not, the Protocols do represent the programme of world revolution, and that in view of their prophetic nature and of their extraordinary resemblance to the protocols of certain secret societies in the past, they were either the work of some such society or of someone profoundly versed in the lore of secret societies who was able to reproduce their ideas and phraseology."[12]

The syllogism is impeccable: since the *Protocols* resemble the story I have told, they confirm it. Or: the *Protocols* confirm the story I have concocted from them; therefore they are true. In the same vein, Rodolphe of Gerolstein, coming from *The Mysteries of Paris* and entering *The Mysteries of the People,* confirms with the authority of the former novel the truth of the latter.

How should we deal with intrusions of fiction into life, now that we have seen the historical impact that this phenomenon can have? I do not wish to propose that my walks in the fictional woods are a remedy for the great tragedies of our time. Nonetheless, these walks have enabled us to understand the mechanisms by which fiction can shape life. At times the results can be innocent and pleasant, as when one goes on a pilgrimage to Baker Street; but at other times life can be transformed into a nightmare instead of a dream. Reflecting on these complex relationships between reader and story, fiction and life, can constitute a form of therapy against the sleep of reason, which generates monsters.

At any rate we will not stop reading fictional stories, because it is in them that we seek a formula to give meaning to our existence. Throughout our lives, after all, we look for a story of our origins, to tell us why we were born and why we have lived. Sometimes we look for a cosmic story, the story of the universe, or for our own personal story (which we tell our confessor or our analyst, or which we write in the pages of a diary). Sometimes our personal story coincides with the story of the universe.

It has happened to me, as the following piece of natural narrative will attest.

Several months ago I was invited to visit the Science Museum of La Coruña, in Galicia. At the end of my visit the curator announced that he had a surprise for me and led me to the planetarium. Planetariums are always suggestive places because when the lights are turned off, one has the impression of being in a desert beneath a starlit sky. But that evening something special awaited me.

Suddenly the room was totally dark, and I could hear a beautiful lullaby by de Falla. Slowly (though slightly faster than in reality, since the presentation lasted fifteen minutes in all) the sky above me began to rotate. It was the sky that had appeared over my birthplace, Alessandria, Italy, on the night of January 5–6, 1932. Almost hyperrealistically, I experienced the first night of my life.

I experienced it for the first time, since I had not seen that first night. Perhaps not even my mother saw it, exhausted as she was after giving birth; but perhaps my father saw it, after quietly stepping out on the terrace, a little restless because of the (to him at least) wondrous event which he had witnessed and which he had jointly caused.

The planetarium used a mechanical device that can be found in a great many places. Perhaps others have had a similar experience. But you will forgive me if during those fifteen minutes I had the impression that I was the only man, since the dawn of time, who had ever had the privilege of being reunited with his own beginning. I was so happy, that I had the feeling—almost the desire—that I could, that I should, die at that very moment, and that any other moment would have been untimely. I would cheerfully have died then, because I had lived through the most beautiful story I had ever read in my entire life. Perhaps I had found the story that we all look for in the pages of books and on the screens of movie theaters: it was a story in which the stars and I were the protagonists. It was fiction because the story had been reinvented by the curator; it was history because it recounted what had happened in the cosmos at a moment in the past; it was real life because I was real, and not the character of a novel. I was, for a moment, the model reader of the Book of Books.

That was a fictional wood I wish I had never had to leave.

But since life is cruel, for you and for me, here I am.

NOTES

INDEX

NOTES

1. ENTERING THE WOODS

1. Italo Calvino, *Six Memos for the Next Millennium* (Cambridge, Mass.: Harvard University Press, 1988).
2. Ibid., p. 36.
3. Ibid., p. 46.
4. Achille Campanile, *Agosto, moglie mia non ti conosco,* in *Opere* (Milan: Bompiani, 1989), p. 830.
5. Carolina Invernizio, *L'albergo del delitto* (Turin: Quartara, 1954), p. 5.
6. Franz Kafka, *"Metamorphosis" and Other Stories,* trans. Willa Muir and Edwin Muir (London: Minerva, 1992), p. 1.
7. Alfred Kazin, *On Native Grounds* (New York: Harcourt Brace, 1982), p. 445.
8. Roger Schank, *Reading and Understanding* (Hillsdale, N.J.: Lawrence Erlbaum, 1982), p. 21.
9. Umberto Eco, *The Role of the Reader* (Bloomington: Indiana University Press, 1979).
10. Umberto Eco, *The Limits of Interpretation* (Bloomington: Indiana University Press, 1990); idem, *Interpretation and Overinterpretation* (Cambridge: Cambridge University Press, 1992).
11. Umberto Eco, "Il tempo di *Sylvie,*" *Poesia e critica* 2 (1962): 51–65; Patrizia Violi, ed., *Sur Sylvie,* special issue of *VS,* 31–32 (January–August, 1982).

12. Gérard de Nerval, *Sylvie: Souvenirs du Valois* (Paris: Editions des Horizons, 1947). Originally published in *La Revue des deux mondes,* 15 July 1853. First published in English as *Sylvie: Recollections of Valois* (New York: George Routledge and Sons, 1887). The two English translations given here are mine.

13. James Joyce, *A Portrait of the Artist as a Young Man* (New York: Viking, 1964), p. 215.

14. On this subject I am particularly indebted to Wayne Booth, *The Rhetoric of Fiction* (Chicago: University of Chicago Press, 1961); Roland Barthes, "Introduction à l'analyse structurale des récits," *Communications* 8 (1966); Tzvetan Todorov, "Les Catégories du récit littéraire," *Communications* 8 (1966); E. D. Hirsch, Jr., *Validity in Interpretation* (New Haven: Yale University Press, 1967); Michael Riffaterre, *Essais de stylistique structurale* (Paris: Flammarion, 1971); idem, *The Semiotics of Poetry* (Bloomington: Indiana University Press, 1978); Gérard Genette, *Figures III* (Paris: Seuil, 1972); Wolfgang Iser, *The Implied Reader* (Baltimore: Johns Hopkins University Press, 1974); Michel Foucault, "What Is an Author?" in Donald F. Bouchard, ed., *Language, Counter-Memory, Practice: Selected Essays and Interviews* (Ithaca: Cornell University Press, 1977); Maria Corti, *An Introduction to Literary Semiotics* (Bloomington: Indiana University Press, 1978); Seymour Chatman, *Story and Discourse* (Ithaca: Cornell University Press, 1978); Charles Fillmore, "Ideal Readers and Real Readers" (mimeo, 1981); Paola Pugliatti, *Lo sguardo nel racconto* (Bologna: Zanichelli, 1985); and Robert Scholes, *Protocols of Reading* (New Haven: Yale University Press, 1989).

15. Iser, *The Implied Reader,* pp. 278–287.

16. Umberto Eco, *The Open Work* (Cambridge, Mass.: Harvard University Press, 1989).

17. Paola Pugliatti, "Reader's Stories Revisited: An Introduction," in *Il lettore: modelli, processi ed effetti dell'interpretazione,* special issue of *VS,* 52–53 (January–May, 1989): 5–6.

18. Wolfgang Iser, *The Act of Reading* (Baltimore: Johns Hopkins University Press, 1976), pp. 34–36.

19. Mickey Spillane, *My Gun Is Quick* (New York: Dutton, 1950), p. 5.

20. According to Gérard Genette, *Seuils* (Paris: Seuil, 1987), the "paratext" consists of the whole series of messages that accompany and help

explain a given text—messages such as advertisements, jacket copy, title, subtitles, introduction, reviews, and so on.

21. See Harold Beaver, commentary on E. A. Poe, *The Narrative of Arthur Gordon Pym* (Harmondsworth: Penguin, 1975), p. 250.

22. Ludwig Wittgenstein, *Philosophical Investigations* (Oxford: Blackwell, 1958), p. 31e.

2. THE WOODS OF LOISY

1. Agatha Christie, *The Murder of Roger Ackroyd,* ch. 27 ("Apologia"), in *Five Classic Murder Mysteries* (New York: Avenel Books, 1985), pp. 301–302.

2. Marcel Proust, "Gérard de Nerval," in *Contre Sainte-Beuve,* trans. Sylvia Townsend Warner, in *Marcel Proust on Art and Literature* (New York: Carroll and Graf, 1984), pp. 147–153.

3. Georges Poulet, *Les métamorphoses du cercle* (Paris: Plon, 1961), p. 255.

4. Gérard Genette, *Narrative Discourse: An Essay in Method,* trans. Jane E. Lewin (Ithaca: Cornell University Press, 1980). On time and narrativity I am particularly indebted to Cesare Segre, *Structure and Time: Narration, Poetry, Models,* trans. John Meddemmen (Chicago: University of Chicago Press, 1979); idem, *Introduction to the Analysis of the Literary Text,* trans. John Meddemmen (Bloomington: Indiana University Press, 1988); Paul Ricoeur, *Time and Narrative,* trans. Kathleen McLaughlin and David Pellauer (Chicago: University of Chicago Press, 1984); and Dorrit Cohn, *Transparent Minds: Narrative Modes for Presenting Consciousness in Fiction* (Princeton: Princeton University Press, 1978).

5. Proust, "Gérard de Nerval," p. 154.

6. On the differences among story, plot, and discourse, I am particularly indebted to Chatman, *Story and Discourse;* Segre, *Structure and Time;* idem, *Introduction to the Analysis of the Literary Text;* Gerald Prince, *Narratology: The Form and Functioning of Narrative* (Berlin: Mouton, 1982); and Mieke Bal, *Narratology: Introduction to the Theory of Narrative,* trans. Christine van Boheemen (Toronto: University of Toronto Press, 1985).

7. T. S. Eliot, "Hamlet," in *Selected Essays* (London: Faber and Faber, 1932), p. 145.

8. Marcel Proust, "A ajouter à Flaubert," in *Contre Sainte-Beuve,* ed. Pierre Clarac (Paris: Gallimard, 1971), p. 300.

3. LINGERING IN THE WOODS

1. Italo Calvino, *Six Memos for the Next Millennium* (Cambridge, Mass.: Harvard University Press, 1988), pp. 35, 46.
2. On inferential walks, see Umberto Eco, *The Role of the Reader* (Bloomington: Indiana University Press, 1979), pp. 31–33.
3. "Scenes We'd Like to See: The Musketeer Who Failed to Get the Girl," in William M. Gaines, *The Bedside "Mad"* (New York: Signet, 1959), pp. 117–121.
4. Isabella Pezzini, "Le passioni del Lector," in Patrizia Magli et al., eds., *Semiotica: Storia, Teoria, Interpretazione—Saggi intorno a Umberto Eco* (Milan: Bompiani, 1992), pp. 227–242.
5. Alessandro Manzoni, *The Betrothed,* trans. Bruce Penman (Harmondsworth: Penguin, 1972), p. 32.
6. See, for instance, works by Seymour Chatman, Gérard Genette, and Gerald Prince.
7. Mickey Spillane, *One Lonely Night* (New York: Dutton, 1950), p. 165.
8. Ian Fleming, *Casino Royale* (London: Glidrose, 1953), ch. 18.
9. Marcel Proust, "A Propos du style de Flaubert," *Nouvelle revue française,* January 1, 1929, p. 950.
10. Gustave Flaubert, *Sentimental Education,* trans. Robert Baldick (Harmondsworth: Penguin, 1964), p. 411.
11. Alexandre Dumas (père), *The Three Musketeers,* anonymous trans. (New York: Grosset and Dunlap, n.d.), pp. 105–107.
12. Dorothy Sayers, introduction to Dante, *The Divine Comedy* (Harmondsworth: Penguin, 1949–1962), p. 9.
13. Dante, *Paradise,* canto 33, verses 55–57, 85–90; trans. Barbara Reynolds, in the Sayers edition, vol. 3 (1962), pp. 344ff.
14. See Umberto Eco, "Narrative Structures in Fleming," in *The Role of the Reader,* pp. 144–174.
15. Manzoni, *The Betrothed,* pp. 25–26.

4. POSSIBLE WOODS

1. John Searle, "The Logical Status of Fictional Discourse," *New Literary History* 14 (1975).
2. Franz Kafka, *"Metamorphosis" and Other Stories,* trans. Willa Muir and Edwin Muir (London: Minerva, 1992), p. 9.
3. Edwin Abbott, *Flatland: A Romance of Many Dimensions* (New York: Dover, 1952; orig. pub. 1884).

4. Lubomir Doležel, "Possible Worlds and Literary Fiction," in Sture Allen, ed., *Possible Worlds in Humanities, Arts, and Sciences: Proceedings of Nobel Symposium 65* (Berlin: De Gruyter, 1989), p. 239.

5. On this point, I am indebted to all the participants at Session 3 of the above-mentioned Nobel Symposium 65, in particular Arthur Danto, Thomas Pavel, Ulf Linde, Gérard Regnier, and Samuel Levin. Other figures of this type can be found in Lionel S. Penrose and Roger Penrose, "Impossible Objects," *British Journal of Psychology* 49 (1958).

6. Umberto Eco, "L'uso pratico del personaggio artistico," in *Apocalittici e integrati* (Milan: Bompiani: 1964).

7. Hilary Putnam, *Representation and Reality* (Cambridge, Mass.: MIT Press, 1988), pp. 22ff.

8. Valentina Pisanty, *Leggere la fiaba* (Milan: Bompiani, 1993), pp. 97–99. The alchemical reading was provided by Giuseppe Sermonti, *Le fiabe del sottosuolo* (Milan: Rusconi, 1989).

5. THE STRANGE CASE OF THE RUE SERVANDONI

1. Lucrecia Escudero, "Malvine: Il Gran Racconto" (Diss.: Università degli Studi di Bologna, Dottorato di Ricerca in Semiotica, 4 Ciclo, 1992).

2. Umberto Eco (in collaboration with Patrizia Violi), "Presuppositions," in *The Limits of Interpretation* (Bloomington: Indiana University Press, 1990), pp. 253–260.

3. I have checked a map of Paris from 1609, on which some of the streets mentioned above do not appear or have different names. In a report entitled *Estat, noms et nombre de toutes les rues de Paris en 1636,* ed. Alfred Franklin (Paris: Léon Willem, 1873; Editions de Paris, 1988), the names given are already those that were used in 1716, according to a map from the latter year that I found. Considering that most maps follow aesthetic criteria and do not show the names of secondary streets, I think that my reconstruction reasonably approximates the situation of the streets in 1625.

4. Keith S. Donnellan, "Reference and Definite Descriptions," *Philosophical Review* 75 (1966): 281–304.

5. Roger C. Schank (with Peter G. Childers), *The Cognitive Computer* (Reading, Mass.: Addison-Wesley, 1984), pp. 81–89.

6. Ibid., p. 83.

7. Ibid., p. 85.

8. Ibid., p. 86.

9. Umberto Eco, "Postscript" to *The Name of the Rose,* trans. William Weaver (New York: Harcourt Brace, 1984).

10. James Joyce, *A Portrait of the Artist as a Young Man* (New York: Viking, 1964), p. 214.

6. FICTIONAL PROTOCOLS

1. Umberto Eco, *The Open Work* (Cambridge, Mass.: Harvard University Press, 1989), p. 264, n. 13.

2. Umberto Eco, *Foucault's Pendulum,* trans. William Weaver (New York: Harcourt Brace, 1988), p. 495.

3. Andrea Bonomi, "Lo spirito della narrazione" (1993, unpublished), ch. 4, quoted with the permission of the author.

4. Theun van Dijk, "Action, Action Description and Narrative," *Poetics* 5 (1974): 287–338.

5. Roland Barthes, "L'Effet de réel," in *Essais critiques IV: Le bruissement de la langue* (Paris: Seuil, 1984), pp. 167–174.

6. Marcel Proust, in *Contre Sainte-Beuve,* trans. Sylvia Townsend Warner, in *Marcel Proust on Art and Literature* (New York: Carroll and Graf, 1984), p. 152.

7. T. S. Eliot, *Selected Essays* (London: Faber and Faber, 1932), p. 144.

8. Jerome Bruner, *Actual Minds, Possible Worlds* (Cambridge, Mass.: Harvard University Press, 1986).

9. See Arthur Danto, *Analytical Philosophy of History* (Cambridge, Mass.: Harvard University Press, 1965); Hayden White, *Metahistory: The Historical Imagination in Nineteenth-Century Europe* (Baltimore: Johns Hopkins University Press, 1973); and Jorge Lozano, *El discurso histórico* (Madrid: Alianza Editorial, 1987).

10. A.-J. Greimas and Joseph Courtés, *Semiotics and Language: An Analytical Dictionary,* trans. Larry Christ and Daniel Patte (Bloomington: Indiana University Press, 1979).

11. For a complete survey of the whole affair see Norman Cohn, *Warrant for Genocide: The Myth of the Jewish World-Conspiracy and the Protocols of the Elders of Zion* (New York: Harper and Row, 1967).

12. Nesta Webster, *Secret Societies and Subversive Movements* (London: Boswell, 1924), pp. 408–409.

Abbott, Edwin: *Flatland*, 79–81, 83, 99

Adam, 129–130

Aesop, 2, 110

Alembert, Jean Le Rond d', 133

Antonioni, Michelangelo: *Blow Up*, 99

Aristotle, 64, 122

Assassins, 134

Augustine, Saint, 68

Austen, Jane, 11

Barruel, Abbé: *Mémoires*, 133–134, 138

Barthes, Roland, 104, 118, 122

Bergman, Ingrid, 127

Berkheim, Charles de, 133

Bible, 68, 128

Black Hundreds, 136, 138

Boccaccio, Giovanni: *Decameron*, 128

Bonomi, Andrea, 118–119

Borges, Jorge Luis, 6, 131; "Funes the Memorious," 110

Bournand, François: *Les Juifs, nos contemporains*, 136

Brotherhood of the Rosy Cross, 132, 138

Bruner, Jerome, 130

Bruno, Giordano, 110

Brutus, 131

Buckingham, Duke of (George Villiers), 64, 90–91, 113

Burke, Kenneth, 129

Calvino, Italo: *If on a Winter's Night a Traveler*, 1–2; *Italian Folkways*, 2–3; *Six Memos for the Next Millennium*, 2–3, 7, 49

Campanile, Achille: *Agosto, moglie mia non ti conosco*, 3–4, 83; *Ma che cos'è questo amore*, 100

Casablanca, 6, 127

Celli, Giorgio, 120–121

Cervantes, Miguel: *Don Quixote,* 127

Charles the Bald, 100

Chatman, Seymour, 54

Childers, Peter: *The Cognitive Computer,* 110–112

Christie, Agatha: *The Murder of Roger Ackroyd,* 27–29

"Cinderella," 84

Coleridge, Samuel Taylor, 75

Collodi, Carlo: *Pinocchio,* 10–11

Columbus, Christopher, 109

Compton-Burnett, Ivy, 64

Condorcet, Marquis de (Marie-Jean Caritat), 133

Confessio roseae crucis, 132

Conrad, Joseph: *Lord Jim,* 127

Corday, Charlotte, 122

Cyon, Elie de, 136, 138

Dake, Charles Romyn, 7

Dali, Salvador, 69

Dante Alighieri: *Divine Comedy,* 66–67, 117, 128

Danto, Arthur, 130

Defoe, Daniel: *Robinson Crusoe,* 123–124

Diderot, Denis, 133

Döblin, Alfred, 84

Doležel, Lubomir, 81–82

Donnellan, Keith, 105

Dostoyevski, Fyodor, 11

Doyle, Arthur Conan, 84, 105, 107, 125, 127, 139

Dreyfus, Alfred, 136

Dumas, Alexandre, 37, 138; *The Count of Monte Cristo,* 64; *Joseph Balsamo,* 135–136; *The Three Musketeers,* 62–64, 90, 101–110, 112–114, 117–118, 126; *Twenty Years Later,* 90–91

Eco, Umberto, 120–121, 140; *Foucault's Pendulum,* 9, 76–77, 86–87, 118; *Interpretation and Overinterpretation,* 10, 108; *Lector in fabula* (*The Role of the Reader*), 1–2, 8, 50; *The Limits of Interpretation,* 10, 95, 108; *The Name of the Rose,* 115, 123; *The Open Work,* 16, 117; "Small Worlds," 95–96; "L'uso pratico del personaggio artistico," 85–86

Einstein, Albert, 5

Elders of Zion, 136–139

Eliot, George (Mary Ann Evans), 14

Eliot, T. S., 36, 127–128, 137

Escudero, Lucrecia, 97

Euclid, 80, 85

Falla, Manuel de, 140

Fama fraternitatis, 132

Faulkner, William: *Sanctuary,* 127

Felton, John, 90–91

Fielding, Henry: *The History of Tom Jones,* 122

Fields, W. C., 122

"Flash Gordon," 92

Flaubert, Gustave: *Madame Bovary,* 36–37, 110–111, 127; *The Sentimental Education,* 56–57, 61

Fleming, Ian, 67–68; *Casino Royale,* 55–56

Frederick the Great, 124

Freemasons, 132–134, 138

Gadda, Carlo Emilio, 118–119

Garibaldi, Giuseppe, 124, 134

Gaudí, Antonio, 77

Genette, Gérard, 30, 54

Gibbon, Edward: *History of the Decline and Fall of the Roman Empire,* 120

Gioberti, Vicenzo, 134
Glaber, Rudolph: *Historia suorum
temporum,* 122–123
Goedsche, Hermann ("John Ret-
cliffe"): *Biarritz,* 135, 138
Goodman, Nelson, 88
Greimas, A.-J., 130
Grimm, Jacob and Wilhelm, 35, 91

"Hansel and Gretel," 27
Hawthorne, Nathaniel: *The Scarlet
Letter,* 124
Hegel, Georg Wilhelm Friedrich,
37, 118
Henry V, 131
Hesse, Hermann: *Siddhartha,* 127
Hitler, Adolf, 137
Homer: *Odyssey,* 33–35, 65
Humblot, M., 49
Huston, John, 36
Huysmans, Joris-Karl, 50

Invernizio, Carolina: *L'albergo del delitto* (*The Murderous Inn*), 4, 86
Ionesco, Eugène, 64
Irving, Washington: "Rip Van Winkle," 95
Iser, Wolfgang: *The Act of Reading,*
16; *The Implied Reader,* 15

Jacobins, 133
James, Henry, 46
Jesuits, 133–135
"Jews, Masters of the World, The,"
135
Joly, Maurice, 135–138
Josephine, Empress, 90
Joyce, James, 117; "The Dead," 36;
Dubliners, 36; *Finnegans Wake,* 16–
17, 109–110, 112; *A Portrait of the
Artist as a Young Man,* 15, 36,

116; *Ulysses,* 6, 27, 33, 59, 84,
117–118, 122, 125, 127
Julius Caesar, 131
Jupiter, 129

Kafka, Franz: "Metamorphosis," 4–
5, 78–79; *The Trial,* 84–85
Kant, Immanuel, 11
Kazin, Alfred, 5
Knights Templars, 77, 132–134, 138
Kuhn, Thomas, 88

Lafayette, Madame de (Marie-
Madeleine Pioche de la Vergne):
La Princesse de Clèves, 123
Lear, Edward, 34–35
Leonardo da Vinci, 11
"Little Red Riding Hood," 6, 8, 27,
34–35, 77, 91–92, 107, 110, 115
Lodwick, Francis, 129
Lovecraft, H. P., 7, 78
Luchet, Marquis de, 133–134, 138
Lucianus of Samosata: *A True Story,*
122

Macaulay, Thomas Babington, 123–
124
Machiavelli, Niccolò, 135
Mad magazine, 50–51
Mani, 134
Mann, Thomas, 5
Manzoni, Alessandro: *I promessi
sposi* (*The Betrothed*), 52–54, 57–
58, 68, 71–73, 78
Mattson, Morris, 20
Medici, 69–70, 85
Melville, Herman: *Moby-Dick,* 20, 27
Michelet, Jules, 134; *Histoire de
France,* 122
Mitchell, Margaret: *Gone with the
Wind,* 88, 90, 92–93, 117–118

Molay, Jacques de, 133
Montesquieu, Baron de (Charles-Louis de Secondat), 135
Musil, Robert: *The Man without Qualities*, 124

Napoleon I (Napoleon Bonaparte), 88–90, 109, 114, 117, 131, 133–134
Napoleon III (Louis-Napoleon), 56, 135–136
Nerval, Gérard de (Gérard Labrunie), 44, 47, 80; *Aurélia*, 15, 32; *Les Filles du feu*, 37; *Sylvie*, 12–15, 20, 22–24, 29–32, 36–43, 54, 65, 68–70, 83–85, 94, 113–114, 117, 125
Neuhaus, Heinrich, 132
Nilus, Sergei, 137–138
Nostradamus (Michel de Nostredame): *Centuries*, 128
Novalis (Friedrich von Hardenberg), 125

Old Man of the Mountain, 134
Ollendorff (publisher), 49

Peckinpah, Sam, 56
Penrose, Lionel S. and Roger, 81
Perec, Georges: *Tentative d'épuisement d'un lieu parisien*, 59–60, 87
Perrault, Charles, 35, 90–91
Pessoa, Fernando, 14
Phaedrus, 2
Philip the Fair, 132
Pisanty, Valentina, 92
Plato: "Cratylus," 129
Plutarch: "Life of Pericles," 123; *Lives*, 122
Poe, Edgar Allan: *The Narrative of Arthur Gordon Pym*, 6–8, 18–21, 28;

"The Philosophy of Composition," 44–47; "The Raven," 44–47
Pollock, Jackson, 59
"Popeye," 127
Poulet, Georges, 29
Protocols of the Learned Elders of Zion, 136–139
Proust, Marcel, 11, 118; "A ajouter à Flaubert," 36–37, 110; *A la Recherche du temps perdu*, 49, 71, 86; *Contre Sainte-Beuve*, 125; "Gérard de Nerval," 29, 32, 38, 43; "A Propos du style de Flaubert," 56–57
Pugliatti, Paola, 16
Putnam, Hilary, 89

Quine, Willard Van Orman, 88
Quinet, Edgar, 134

Rabelais, François: *Gargantua*, 117, 127
Rachkovsky, Peter Ivanovich, 136, 138
Radcliffe, Ann: *The Mysteries of Udolpho*, 95–96, 101
Radiguet, Raymond: *Le Diable au corps*, 11
Readcliff, John, 136, 138
Robbe-Grillet, Alain: *La Maison de rendez-vous* (*The House of Assignation*), 81–82
Rocky Horror Picture Show, The, 127–128
Roothaan, Father, 135
Rosicrucians, 132–133, 138
Rostand, Edmond: *Cyrano de Bergerac*, 126
Rousseau, Jean-Jacques, 31, 69, 85

Salinger, J. D., 11
Sayers, Dorothy, 66

Schank, Roger: *The Cognitive Computer,* 110–112; *Reading and Understanding,* 5–6
Schwarz, Berthold, 43–44
Scott, Walter, 120; *Ivanhoe,* 94–95
Scottish Freemasons, 132–134
Searle, John, 75
Servandoni, Giovanni Niccolò, 104, 107, 114
Shakespeare, William, 117; *Hamlet,* 88, 127–128, 137
Simonini, Captain, 134, 138
Southern Literary Messenger, 19
Spillane, Mickey, 61; *My Gun Is Quick,* 17; *One Lonely Night,* 55–56
Stagecoach, 49
Stendhal (Marie-Henri Beyle): *Le Rouge et le noir* (*The Red and the Black*), 85–86, 117
Sterne, Laurence: *Tristram Shandy,* 7–8
Stevenson, Robert Louis: *Treasure Island,* 127
Stout, Rex, 84, 93–94, 114
Sturges, John: *Bad Day at Black Rock,* 64–65

Sue, Eugène, 136, 138; *The Mysteries of Paris,* 135, 139; *The Mysteries of the People,* 134–135, 139; *The Wandering Jew,* 134
Swift, Jonathan: *Gulliver's Travels,* 14

Tolstoy, Leo: *War and Peace,* 93
"Tom Thumb," 27
Tracy, Spencer, 64–65
Turgot, Anne-Robert-Jacques, 133

Ulysses (Odysseus), 33–34

Verne, Jules, 7; *Around the World in Eighty Days,* 54
Virgil: *Aeneid,* 128
Vittorio Emanuele III, 75, 77–78
Voltaire (François-Marie Arouet), 133

Wagner, Richard, 58
Warhol, Andy, 59
Wayne, John, 49
Webster, Nesta: *Secret Societies and Subversive Movements,* 138